HOW TO SUCCEED
in the
GAME
of LIFE

34 INTERVIEWS WITH THE **WORLD'S** GREATEST COACHES

CHRISTIAN KLEMASH

Andrews McMeel
Publishing, LLC

Kansas City

06 07 08 09 10 11 RR4 10 9 8 7 6 5 4 3 2 1

Library of Congress Cataloging-in-Publication Data
Klemash, Christian.
    How to succeed in the game of life : 34 interviews with the world's greatest coaches / Christian Klemash.
        p. cm.
    ISBN-13: 978-0-7407-6065-5
    ISBN-10: 0-7407-6065-3
        1. Coaches (Athletics)—United States—Interviews. 2. Coaching (Athletics)—Philosophy. 3. Success. I. Title.

    GV697.A1K565 2006
    796.07'7—dc22

                                                                          2006042827

www.andrewsmcmeel.com

Attention: Schools and Businesses
Andrews McMeel books are available at quantity discounts with bulk purchase for educational, business, or sales promotional use. For information, please write to: Special Sales Department, Andrews McMeel Publishing, LLC, 4520 Main Street, Kansas City, Missouri 64111.

This is dedicated to my father,
the world's greatest coach.

To Roe,
Wishing you success
in all you do!
Happy Holidays,
Christine Klemst

12·10·06

CONTENTS

ACKNOWLEDGMENTS

This book is the result of the hard work and cooperation of many people. I'd like to thank all of the coaches who shared their time, experience, and wisdom with me; Alec MacDonald and Danielle Egan-Miller at Browne & Miller Literary Associates, for believing in me and this project; Josh Brewster; Katie Anderson, and Andrews McMeel Publishing, for giving us a shot; Jennifer Potter, for all of her help; my cousin Jimmy, for his endless enthusiasm and input; and my wife, Jennifer, for holding down the fort while I got this done.

Believe in yourself so much
that you counter others' disbelief.

—TRUDI LACEY

INTRODUCTION

I am a pretty typical guy, a couch potato who grew up watching sports on television like most American boys. I primarily watched the big four—football, baseball, basketball, and hockey—along with boxing and a few select Olympic events, like figure skating (though I'll deny that at my neighborhood bar). So I was thrilled when, over the past couple of years, I had an opportunity to live out any sports fanatic's dream: to speak with some of the greatest coaches ever and pick their brains about what it takes to succeed.

In 2001, after thirteen years of living in Los Angeles and pursuing a career as an actor and screenwriter, I returned to my hometown of Philadelphia because:

1) The Internet company I worked for was closing their Los Angeles office.
2) I had not yet reached Tom Cruise status as an actor.
3) I had recently rekindled a romance with a woman from Philly while back East on Christmas vacation (we're now married).
4) My bitterness at the movie industry was growing (see reason No. 2).

I grew up in south Philadelphia, a blue-collar section of the city, which is home to some of the most loyal and rabid fans in the country. Philly sports fans measure up well to the Red Sox faithful in Boston, the Cubs diehards in Chicago, and the silver-and-black army of the Oakland Raiders. Hollywood has a lot of other entertainment distractions and I was looking forward to once again living in a city that is crazy about sports.

When I came back, I needed a job to keep me afloat. The Internet bubble of the late 1990s had just burst and I was having trouble finding work in the computer industry. Luckily, a childhood friend got me a job as a suite attendant at the local sports arena, the Wachovia Center, where the Sixers and Flyers play. Since the money was decent and I love sports, it was a good fit. I worked there for a full season and attended games almost every night, and that's when I got the idea for this book.

I realized how many different teams and players I had seen over the years. Some of them (outside of Philadelphia) had sustained periods of excellence. The obvious examples are the New York Yankees, the Boston Celtics, the Dallas Cowboys, and the Montreal Canadiens, along with the Michael Jordan–era Chicago Bulls and the San Francisco 49ers of the 1980s and early 1990s. These organizations consistently produced winners. Since I was watching games on a nightly basis now, I became intrigued by what made certain teams and players so successful, as opposed to most of the other teams in the leagues. What made one team or person more successful than another?

Well, I certainly didn't have the expertise and experience to answer this question, but I knew who would. Coaches are the authority on this subject. They are directly responsible for the success of the team as a whole, and on a more personal level, the individuals themselves. Since they devote their lives to teaching others about cooperation, character, and winning, they have a firm grip on the elements needed to build and sustain success. They've worked with a wide spectrum of players, from the least to the most talented, and have used a variety of tactics to bring out the best in different kinds of athletes. In addition, they're constantly being scrutinized by their superiors and the public, so they know what it's like to handle pressure. If their teams don't produce, they're fired. Therefore, I thought they could shed some light on what it takes to make the most successful individuals and the best teams, so I set out to interview the greatest coaches in the sporting world.

I put together a list of questions about what elevated certain teams and individuals above others and began mailing requests to coaches throughout the country. Weeks and months went by without a reply from anyone. Then several decline letters started trickling in. I was losing hope for this book when one day I received a positive response from legendary UCLA basketball coach John Wooden. Coach Wooden had actually taken the time to write out answers to my questions, included his telephone number, and mailed the letter back to me. He also included an autographed picture and a copy of his famed "Pyramid of Success." I was thrilled when I received his letter! I called him immediately and he graciously granted me a telephone interview. Coach Wooden had breathed new life into my project.

Riding the energy from the John Wooden interview, and armed with his advice of patience and persistence, I came up with a new strategy to approach the coaches for interviews. I called one coach after another, keeping a log and following up on unreturned calls every couple of weeks. I was methodical and persistent, often waiting months for a reply, understanding how extremely busy these men and women were. Scotty Bowman took nine months to get back to me. Bill Walsh took over a year, as did Bill Parcells. Several teams declined my original request, but granted me an interview more than a year later. The New York Yankees, for example, originally declined my interview request with Joe Torre in November 2003. However, when I requested it again in February 2005, Mr. Torre kindly accepted.

As the book progressed, I spoke with coaches I never dreamed I would, and glimpsed a side of them you don't see on television. When I was trying to schedule Whitey Herzog, he postponed the interview a couple of times to go fishing with his buddies; he said he preferred fishing to doing interviews. Who can blame him? When I asked for Angelo Dundee on the phone, he bellowed in his East Coast accent, "You got him!" Mr. Dundee is from the same neighborhood that I grew up in, so we had a lot to talk about. We discussed Muhammad Ali, Sugar Ray Leonard, and Roberto Duran—all idols of my youth.

In a short amount of time I felt as comfortable with Mr. Dundee as I would with any guy from my block.

Another time, I was on the phone with a friend when my call-waiting rang. I clicked over to the other line and a gravelly voice on the other end said, "Bill Cowher calling for Christian Klemash." I had requested the interview with Coach Cowher a couple of weeks earlier and he just called me out of the blue. I clicked back to my friend and told him I'd have to call him back because Bill Cowher was on the line—he couldn't believe it and neither could I.

I'm still a little shocked that I spoke with all of these great coaches, and I'm truly grateful that they shared their time, knowledge, and experience with me. The advice they gave me has helped me realize a dream of my own in writing this book. I'm sure it will help and inspire you to achieve some of your own dreams!

CHAPTER ONE

DEFINING SUCCESS

When I returned home in April 2001, the Philadelphia 76ers were about to make an exciting run through the play-offs. The series was exciting, with the Allen Iverson–led Sixers being pushed to the brink of elimination twice, in seven-game affairs against Vince Carter and the Toronto Raptors in the second round, and against Ray Allen and the Milwaukee Bucks in the Eastern Conference Finals.

In the championship, my hometown Sixers met my "former hometown" Los Angeles Lakers, with Shaquille O'Neal and Kobe Bryant. After the Sixers won Game 1 in Los Angeles, the Lakers swept the next four games en route to their second straight NBA Championship.

When I watched the television coverage and listened to the radio commentary about the series, I was a little concerned. Most of the hosts and listeners talked about what a great season it had been, and they seemed completely satisfied with the outcome. If you didn't know that the Sixers had lost, you would think they had just won the title, but I saw it differently. I knew the Sixers were underdogs, and I knew it would have been an enormous upset if they had beaten Los Angeles—but I wasn't happy they'd lost. I thought the Sixers had a nice season, but were in fact crushed in the championship by a superior team. There was room to improve and maybe an acquisition or two to be made so that next time they could better match up against the powerful O'Neal.

However, in the media, talk continually centered around what a great season we had had and how no one expected the Sixers would beat the mighty Lakers. Maybe people were focusing on the positive, but this attitude angered me. I hate the Lakers. Even when I was living there I hated them, with all of their movie stars and glitz and glamour. I called in to Philly's sports radio station and expressed my thoughts on-air about how Philadelphia seemed to have become "easily pleased." The host hung up on me.

Now I'm rational enough to know that my thoughts really can't make a team win or lose, but I think if an entire city accepts losing, you're setting yourself up for failure. My point is that when I was growing up, it was only considered a successful season if we *won* the championship. Since I left, however, expectations had diminished.

And so the question for this chapter came into my mind: How would Vince Lombardi define a successful season? What about John Wooden? Bill Parcells? Red Auerbach?

When applied to life, the question takes on much broader possibilities, so I did not specify whether I was speaking in professional terms or in a more general sense. Most of the coaches, however, focused on the bigger picture and gave answers directed at succeeding in life.

One of the responses that jumped out at me was when Emanuel Steward laughed and said that, financially speaking, he thought he had achieved success when he could go to a restaurant and not have to look at the prices on the menu any longer, because he could then afford to order whatever he wanted.

The coaches' most common theme was reaching one's potential as a person; in other words, when a person gives their best effort and maximizes their ability, that's success. They talked about the process of achieving and maintaining success by improving and trying to get better every day. Their definitions of success helped me reshape my idea of success, organize my goals better, focus on day-to-day tasks, and put in my best efforts.

In that sense, I guess the Sixers' season could be considered successful because they did maximize their potential, and simply lost to a better team. I can live with that. Living with another Lakers' championship was a little harder to accept.

How would you define success?

RED AUERBACH

"There are two kinds of success. There's success in your own eyes and there's success in the eyes of other people. If you want to feel successful in your own eyes, you gotta feel satisfied with your life, satisfied with your accomplishments. That's success.

"The success in the minds of other people is them thinking, 'Hey, he won a championship and he's a very successful coach'—when you in your own mind might feel a little bit insecure."

Red Auerbach should feel satisfied with his accomplishments. He is the most accomplished coach and executive in NBA history, winning a total of sixteen championships—nine as a head coach and another seven after moving to the front office.

DUSTY BAKER

"Success, I think, can't be defined necessarily by what the public classifies in terms of success. You need to have satisfaction on the inside—that's what success is.

"It's not necessarily prosperity. It's reaching a goal and then continuing to have goals after you reach them. I asked Sadaharu Oh years ago, through an interpreter, what motivated him. He was a nine-time MVP. And I asked him if he was satisfied with his success. He said you should never be satisfied while you are active and still pursuing your career. You should not feel too successful until after your career is over; you should always continue to strive to be better."

Sadaharu Oh is the all-time professional baseball home run king with 868 career home runs. He led the Japanese major leagues in home runs fifteen times and was league MVP nine times. He was noted for taking thirty to forty minutes of batting practice a day, and he is considered a living legend in his native Japan.

BRIAN BILLICK

"First of all, it's just that—you have to define your definition of success. Because there's always going to be somebody who thinks that you could do it better or differently. Whether it's winning the Super Bowl, or leading the league in a certain category, there's always going to be a different opinion.

"But for me it clearly is maximizing the talent that you have, whether it's personally or on a team. Even compared to the 2000 Super Bowl year, there are those who might intimate that my best coaching job may well have been in 2002 with a 7–9 football team— it was the youngest team in the National Football League—because of what we were able to accomplish. However, as modest as a 7–9 record sounds, considering who we did it with and under what circumstances—the lack of a quarterback, Ray Lewis got hurt—you'd have to look at that year as a successful year."

Coach Billick is a tough guy and mentioned a couple of times that he thought he was considered arrogant or egotistical by the media. He believes that the 2002 season was every bit as meaningful as the 2000 Super Bowl–winning season. He also believes that his team's effort is a direct reflection of his coaching staff and this validates his own success, just as much as his most successful year, since the 2002 team did not have as much talent and still hung in to compete.

NICK BOLLETTIERI

"Success to me is having accomplished something, then going and accomplishing something else, and then when you do that, you accomplish something else. But each time you try to have more success, you go to zones of life that people only dream of.

"Success is beating the success you've had and really putting yourself out on a limb where only a few people would ever take that chance. Success is continued success, meaning along the way you're gonna have ups and downs, but over time, the pendulum keeps going up and up and up. That's why only a few people make the big time and climb the highest of mountains. That, to me, is success."

Although Coach Bollettieri is well known for coaching child prodigies like Andre Agassi, Anna Kournikova, and Maria Sharapova, he believes that one should never cease striving for success at any age, proceeding on to say . . .

"And success continues until the day you die. Whether you're forty, fifty, sixty, seventy, or eighty years old. Mother Teresa at eighty-seven years old, John Glenn at seventy-eight—that's success."

Even in his seventies, Bollettieri still runs his academy and coaches on a daily basis.

BOBBY BOWDEN

"Number one, success to me would have to be built on my spiritual beliefs. This gets into my religion. I believe in life after death. I believe in a term called "saved." I believe in a term called "savior." And to me, I will still not be a success unless when I go, I go to the good place. It goes back to that scripture that says, 'What if a man gains the whole world but loses his soul?'

"That's the ultimate success. That determines what success really is. Now there's successes on earth, like winning the ball game, or making a lot of money, or marrying a beautiful woman, but if I had only one answer to give, it'd be eternal success."

Coach Bowden is a deeply religious, fundamentalist Southern Baptist. He paraphrases Matthew 16:26 here: "What shall it profit a man if he gains the whole world and loses his own soul?"

SCOTTY BOWMAN

"Well, success comes in different stages, but I think it's doing what you enjoy doing. If you enjoy your work, to me, that's as successful as anything. There are other measurements of success, which are naturally wins and losses, finances, and a lot of other things, but I think that a person who gets to do something that is hardly even work to them, even though it's a job, is the most successful. You're pretty successful if you end up doing something you enjoy doing."

Scotty Bowman has been involved in hockey since he played as a young boy in the 1930s. His first full-time coaching job began in 1956 and he went on to coach for nearly the next half century (until 2002). Even after his retirement, Bowman remains employed as a consultant by the Detroit Red Wings organization. He has spent a lifetime inside the game he truly loves.

JOHN CHANEY

"If you find yourself being stimulated, being challenged, being driven, being pushed, inspired, influenced, and also encouraged—when anybody is in a position that any of those things can happen to them or to a group, then that is success.

"When you reach the stage where you feel complete, where you feel as though you have accomplished as much as you were given an opportunity to accomplish. If you can reach that stage where you feel every morning, every day, that you've given your best, that kind of success becomes not just objective, but it becomes subjective because you know that you've given your best.

"I always say to my guys, 'The most important day of your life is today. This very minute is the most important minute of your life. You must win this minute. You must win this day. And tomorrow will take care of itself.'"

Chaney prides himself on being a teacher of life as well as of basketball. Interestingly, while at Cheyney State in 1979 he was awarded the State of Pennsylvania Distinguished Faculty Award for his mesmerizing lectures on life.

BILL COWHER

"I think success should be measured by, number one, making sure you're happy—not what someone is able to accomplish monetarily. There are a lot of people that may be making a lot of money but I'm not so sure how happy they are and how successful they are.

"I think it's finding happiness, and how many people you touch along the way. How many people you can leave your impression on. To me, that's a successful person—someone who can be a part of someone else's development, is happy with what they're doing, and has a passion for what they're doing. And that's not always easy for people—to be able to have a life where they're doing something that they truly love to do.

"So I think it's to find true happiness and touch people along the way."

Coach Cowher showed a softer side with this comment, contrary to the strong, forceful persona he is often associated with.

ANNE DONOVAN

"Success to me is the satisfaction of knowing that I've been prepared, I've done absolutely everything I could do that's in my control to be prepared. And I guess part of success is being committed to enjoying the process. So for me that's success. . . . I mean, we happen to be on top of the WNBA right now, but success is more than the wins. It's going through the process with people that I care about and people that are committed to the same things I'm committed to."

Coach Donovan's teams are among the best prepared and most adaptable in the league. In 2004, the Seattle Storm lost the first game of the WNBA Finals, only to come back and win the final two games and capture their first WNBA Championship.

ANGELO DUNDEE

"This is the key to success: You gotta have fun. If you don't have fun at it, you should get out of it."

As Muhammad Ali's trainer, Angelo was an insider on a team that revolutionized boxing and boxing promotion. Ali was unlike any fighter before him, joking and trading jabs with the press. He recited his own poetry and often picked the rounds where he thought he'd knock out opponents. Along with Bundini Brown, Muhammad Ali and Angelo Dundee mastered the art of fight promotion and appreciated the entertainment aspect of boxing more than any team before or since.

TONY DUNGY

"I would define success as doing the absolute best that you are capable of doing. That's not the same as winning every game—it's being as good as you could possibly be. And if you do that, I think you're successful."

Tony Dungy maximized his abilities to turn himself into a professional athlete. As a defensive back, he made up for his lack of size, speed, and power by studying game films and analyzing his opponents. His mental approach and expansive knowledge allowed him to anticipate other teams' moves before they happened, giving him the edge he needed to excel. This work ethic and preparation has made him one of the best coaches in the NFL.

HERMAN EDWARDS

"I think for me, success in life has nothing to do with what you gain and accomplish for yourself, it's really what you do for others that matters."

Coach Edwards supports numerous charities and he hosts the Annual Herman Edwards Charity Golf Classic, which benefits the Boys and Girls Club in Seaside, California, where he grew up.

JEFF FISHER

"I'd say that the hardest part of success is that you have to keep on being successful. You can't just flash. We're being evaluated day by day, week by week, game by game, year after year. So you want to avoid the flash. You want to strive to establish a winning expectation and maintain it.

"It goes way beyond establishing that ultimate goal. What's more important is establishing the short-term goals and knocking them off one at a time, as you work toward the ultimate goal."

From 2000 to 2004, Tennessee amassed more regular-season wins than any team in the NFL. Coach Fisher led his team to the play-offs in 1999, 2000, 2002, and 2003.

DAN GABLE

"I look at what impact you as a person have in society. And when the people that I directly influence go out and influence other people for the positive and good, I think success has been accomplished.

"In your own family, when you turn people out who are contributing in society, it eventually grows into huge numbers. Whatever profession you're in, look at the number of people you've had the opportunity to work with and see what they're doing now, and if they're doing a lot of the same stuff that was important to you, then I think that is success. It could be the number-thirty person on a squad, but when you look and see what they are doing, if they're making a positive contribution, that's success."

Coach Gable has produced an unprecedented number of wrestling disciples. In fact, a number of them have gone on to become head wrestling coaches at some of America's top universities and the USA national team, such as:

Terry Brands of USA Wrestling
Tom Brands of Virginia Tech
Tim Cysewski of Northwestern University
Barry Davis of the University of Wisconsin
Duane Goldman of the University of Indiana
Brad Penrith of Northern Iowa University
Jim Zalesky of the University of Iowa
Lennie Zalesky of Cal Davis
Mark Johnson of the University of Illinois

BRAD GILBERT

"Trying to get better everyday."

This simple premise is the foundation of Gilbert's coaching philoso- phy. According to Andy Roddick, "Brad's influence has been huge. He just knows what to say and when to say it. He makes it so simple, and that's what I need."

Gilbert said of Roddick, "At twenty-one, he's got to get way better. If he doesn't, he won't win a bunch of majors. I used to tell Andre [Agassi] that [baseball icon] Barry Bonds was my hero because of the way he improved even beyond the age of thirty-five. That's why

Andre thinks he can still get better and why I'd like to think Andy is nowhere near the level he's going to reach."

CARRIE GRAF

"Even for someone that's involved with high-level sports, in terms of success in life—we often mistake it for winning things and achieving things. We forget to stop and smell the roses and understand what a successful life can be, regardless of achievements related to other people. Success in family life, success in social life."

The first part of Coach Graf's answer to this question was Ralph Waldo Emerson's quote about a garden patch and a healthy child. She recited a portion of the deeply moving quote by heart, which was quite impressive, but this combined with her answer really conveyed the strong feelings she had about having a successful life in the larger picture as opposed to professionally. (The Emerson quote is included in the favorite quotes chapter of this book.)

APRIL HEINRICHS

"I have to steal a quote from Warren Beatty who said, 'I'm not sure of what the definition of success is, but I think it's when you're uncertain as to whether what you're doing is work or a hobby.'

"And for me, success has very little to do with winning. I fight the conflict and contradiction at times, because I am hired as the technical director and head coach of the U.S. Olympic National Team to win games. I am evaluated based on winning games and I reject that. It's in some ways sort of ironic that I am where I am, because I don't believe people should be evaluated on whether you win or lose in sports. In business it might be a little bit different because you can control more of the variables, but in sports, the ball bounces, the weather changes, the referee has good performances and poor performances, and your opponent does various things.

"So my definition of success is truly based on the level of satisfaction I get at what I do. The level of satisfaction I get from setting goals and achieving them, and setting goals and seeing the progress. Setting goals and stumbling sometimes, but having to reevaluate or restructure goals. Success is always measured in my journey."

Coach Heinrichs's journey in soccer has spanned three decades. Known as a tenacious competitor, she was named female player of the 1980s by Soccer America *magazine, won the World Cup as a player in 1991, and coached the U.S. Women's Team to Olympic gold in 2004. In 2005, Coach Heinrichs stepped down as coach of the U.S. team, but continued on as a consultant.*

WHITEY HERZOG

"People define success in different ways. I think I'm successful by the fact that I'm a grandfather. I have nine grandchildren—eight boys and one girl. I have eight healthy grandsons from ages twenty-one to three. One of them just signed with the Yankees. He's playing in Staten Island. Another one just came back from Afghanistan. I think that's success, the fact that when we have the Fourth of July or when we have Christmas, Labor Day, or Thanksgiving celebrations, when they come to see me, their grandpa—I feel pretty good about that.

"I think that having your health, having your friends—that's success. Success is having a lot of good friends. Success is having a wonderful family. And I have both."

Whitey Herzog lives where he managed for most of his career, in his hometown of St. Louis, surrounded by family and friends.

In 2004, Herzog's grandson John Urick led the Battle Creek Yankees with 15 home runs and became one of their primary run producers as he racked up 65 RBIs in 396 at bats.

KEN HITCHCOCK

"For me, success as a coach is getting your team to act and behave as one. That to me is a compliment, when somebody says, 'Boy, your team plays like a team.' That's success, because that means that you're acting and behaving as one and you're behaving as a championship group. It's a good feeling, a really good feeling.

"Individually, I don't really think I'm that successful, because I don't really pause to think about that. I'm too busy climbing every mountain. Once one mountain gets climbed I want to go to another one. I don't really pause and reflect. I'm not one of these guys who puts up a bunch of pictures and has a bunch of photocopies of trophies and championships—I'm not really one of those people that does that.

"Sometimes that's a fault, but I have pictures in my office of people I've met in my life or things that I value, but nothing really regarding our sport. So I don't really think of myself as a successful person, I just think of myself as a coach that's trying to get better every day."

Coach Hitchcock has a low-key approach that really comes across in the way he speaks. He hardly ever raises his voice and has a true humility that's reflected in the comment above.

BELA KAROLYI

"Success is an attitude. It is something you are working toward from the very first step. In my profession it is definitely an attitude, driving you toward success. An attitude working day in and day out that you are sharing and influencing and motivating with your partner or student. Through this you get to work toward a common goal. That is success."

Coach Karolyi's energetic, winning attitude comes across in everything he says. He is one of those special people who says, "You can do it!" and you believe it.

TRUDI LACEY

"I would define success as staying true to yourself. Defining who you are. Living to your higher power, and encouraging and empowering other people to do the same."

Coach Lacey's spirituality was evident throughout our interview. She always has her eye on the larger picture and believes her true calling is to help people and motivate others to become their best self.

MARVIN LEWIS

"Preparation. Accomplishing your goals through preparation."

When Coach Lewis was hired by the Cincinnati Bengals, he employed this approach, declaring, "We're going to hammer home competition, preparation, and diligence in everything we're going to do. We're going to learn how to study. We're going to learn how to meet. Everything we do we're going to be professionals, and that's going to come out on Sunday."

LUTE OLSON

"Being the best you can be, regardless of what it is that you do. And a person needs to be passionate about what they do because that's the only way you're going to be happy: if you have a passion for what you do."

TOM OSBORNE

"Well, I've been struck by Stephen Covey's book *The Seven Habits of Highly Effective People.* Somewhere in the start of that book he talks about the fact that he had reviewed all the literature he could find concerning success over the history of our country, and he noticed that during the first 150 years or so, up until somewhere around World War II, success was defined primarily in terms of character traits.

"A successful person worked hard, was honest, was loyal, was generous, was kind. And he said that since World War II, the last fifty years or so, success has been defined primarily in terms of material possessions, power, and prestige. And I guess I was struck with that statement because I believe it's very true.

"I'm old enough now that I can remember the general ethic of the people coming out of the 1930s, the Depression. People who were in debt would make unbelievable sacrifices to pay off that debt, whereas today people would in many cases declare bankruptcy and walk away. And that has really concerned me because I think our definition of success has gravitated toward economic considerations and prestige and power. And certainly here in Washington, D.C., many times the measure of success is power, you know—whether or not you're a committee chairman—as long as you're in a position to make some significant changes.

"So I guess my definition of success would hinge more on doing the best you can with what you have. Having good character, a good work ethic, integrity. That doesn't necessarily mean that you make a lot of money or that you ever attain a position of power.

"I think also success has to do a lot with your family. Staying married to one person for your lifetime. Now certainly there are some people who are very successful who don't, and maybe some reasons why marriages fail, but for the most part, you don't walk away from your responsibilities, you don't walk away from your family. I would define success more in those ways."

The Seven Habits of Highly Effective People, which was published in 1990, is a hugely popular self-help book that guides people to become "effective" through principles of character.

BILL PARCELLS

"That's pretty easy for me. I would say that success is never final, but failure can be. In my business, success is never going to satisfy anybody. It's only a temporary gratification. They're gonna want more. So I've learned to deal with that. You have to go forward.

"No matter what you achieve, you've gotta move forward. It's gotta be onward and upward because it's not final. You can go from being pretty successful to pretty downtrodden and you can do it very quickly, particularly in this business."

Coach Parcells's career has been a true case study in continual success. He won two Super Bowls with the New York Giants in 1986 and 1991. Then he moved on to take the New England Patriots to the Super Bowl in 1997. In 1998, he guided the New York Jets to the AFC Championship game, and he guided his fourth team, the Dallas Cowboys, to the play-offs in 2004.

MIKE SCIOSCIA

"I think success is really just achieving your potential as a person. Whatever that potential is—to have it materialize and become achievement, I think, is success.

"Some of the toughest things to watch along the way (and I know it happens in all walks of life) is to watch people with incredible potential that don't realize it enough to where it becomes achievement. That's one of the toughest things. I think if you do get to that level, I consider that success.

"We're not all gonna set world records, we're not all gonna be all-stars, we're not all gonna become first in our class at Harvard Law, you know. Not that that shouldn't be a goal of yours, but the more pragmatic approach is to say, 'This is what I have, let me get to the level that I can achieve.' And that's when you look back and you're satisfied with the way things have gone. If you've maximized what your potential is, that's success."

Scioscia's comments mirror his own attributes and playing style. He made the most out of his ability by becoming one of the game's best defensive catchers, and his steady presence and game-management skills behind the plate have transferred seamlessly to the dugout.

TUBBY SMITH

"To me it's the satisfaction within each individual that they've given their best effort. That you did all you could. You did the right thing. You felt like in your heart, in your mind, in your soul, that you have done your best.

"Because we all have the potential to do certain things, to reach certain goals. So when you look back on it, if you didn't win the game or get the job, you're gonna ask why. Why did this happen, or why didn't this happen?

"To me success is mutual. It's when you can say, 'Hey, I did my job. I did what I was supposed to do. I did all that I could do.'

"My dad used to tell me, 'Boy, you don't have to be no hero. I don't expect you to do all this work in one day.' He'd give an assignment and he'd expect me to finish it, though. And that's all anybody asks. It's like drills in practice, you don't have to kill yourself—just finish the play. But some kids, they look for ways to get around things, to avoid them. That's what unsuccessful people do."

Coach Smith knows about finishing assignments. He is the sixth of seventeen children raised on a rural farm in southern Maryland, and often had to help harvest produce and do other manual chores as required by his father, a military man.

EMANUEL STEWARD

"From a financial viewpoint, success is when you can go to a restaurant and only look at the left side of the menu. To me, that's financial success. It's a simple little phrase, but to me it means a lot. I never want to know what the price is—if I want it, that's what I'm gonna order.

"And the spiritual point of it is when a person has reached whatever his potential is in life and he feels very good about himself and is satisfied with where he falls in the composition of people in his profession. To be considered the top this or that, or maybe number three or number two—that's success. In some cases, like me, I'm never satisfied until I'm number one at everything I do. Success is different for different people."

Coach Steward worked his way from a poor southern childhood in West Virginia, through the rough streets of Detroit, and on to become the most successful trainer in boxing history. He can now afford to order whatever he wants at any restaurant in the world.

JOE TORRE

"I think it's all from within and I've learned that. It's how you feel about yourself. The thing that I've learned more than anything is how to talk to people. And it's not fair to feel that if you don't wear a World Series ring, you haven't gotten to where you need to be or you shouldn't feel good about yourself. Because it wasn't until after I got one that I realized that not everyone gets the opportunity to do that. And they shouldn't feel the way I felt.

"To me, success is getting the most out of your ability. It's being able to go past that wall where you feel tired and frustrated. And once you go beyond that wall I think there's a great deal of pride involved. Life isn't easy and if you just sit down when you get tired instead of pushing on, then I don't think you ever realize satisfaction and self-esteem."

Mr. Torre mentioned the void he felt from not winning a World Series as a player several times. He said that being surrounded by players that had won the Series made him feel somewhat inferior. He persevered though, and after being fired twice as a manager (with the Braves in 1984 and Cardinals in 1995), he was hired by the New York Yankees, where he has won four Series rings.

JOHN TORTORELLA

"Defining success is looking at the ultimate goal, setting your goal as a team or an individual, going through the process of the ups and downs of trying to attain that goal, and finally, getting it done.

"Success isn't the final winning of the Stanley Cup or getting the thing done that you wanted to do as an individual in your business, but success is handling all of the ups and downs from A to B to get to that spot. That's what defines success—how you handle those situations within the time frame to get the final result. The final result isn't success, it's how you handle all those situations to get there."

In 2004, John Tortorella led the Tampa Bay Lightning to their ultimate goal by winning the first Stanley Cup in franchise history. Along the way, the Lightning handled the ups and downs of two excruciating seven-game series, defeating the Philadelphia Flyers in the conference finals and the Calgary Flames in the championship round to claim the title.

DICK VERMEIL

"I think number one would be being really happy with inner peace. I don't think it has anything to do with money. True happiness doesn't. I think it has to do with inner peace with yourself and how it directly reflects to your family."

BILL WALSH

"Success is progress. It's becoming better at what you do. That's what I always emphasize with the players, that if you can improve your skills and take advantage of it, that's success. I don't necessarily measure it in winning and losing, although that's always a factor. But if you've improved, that's success.

"For example, our team in 1980 had six wins and ten losses. But during that year we improved every week, to the point that when the next season started we became world champions. So success really started then—while we were losing, we were improving."

Coach Walsh continued talking about the 1981 team that eventually won their first Super Bowl . . .

"After we played ten or twelve games we then began to look at the possibility of running the table. Prior to that we were just in survival mode, trying to win every week and just survive. But at some point during that season we began to beat the best teams in football and then we thought we would have a chance. But we didn't think about the Super Bowl until we beat Dallas in that playoff game. You just don't have time to dream away when you have a real tough challenge ahead of you."

LENNY WILKENS

"If you look in the dictionary, it says that success is something achieved, that one has sought and pursued. But to me, I work with people, and if you help people to be better, to accomplish something, to succeed at something, then I think you see some success, and that's not easy to do. Of course in professional sports we're all measured by how many games we win, but there's more to it than that. You watch young people and see them mature and function as human beings in society, as productive people, where they're giving back. That's success."

Lenny Wilkens has been helping people his entire life. As a player he was chosen by his peers as a representative for the players association and helped initiate the first pension plan for NBA players. He has been actively involved in a number of charities throughout the country, from the Odessa Brown Children's Clinic in Seattle, which provides medical and dental care for low-income families, to the Atlanta Center for Abused Children.

JOHN WOODEN

"Success, to me, is peace of mind, which is a direct result of self-satisfaction in knowing you made the effort to become the best of which you were capable. Success is coming as close as possible to reaching your maximum potential at whatever task you're involved in."

Coach Wooden's wisdom and knowledge come across in everything he says. His statement is the culmination of his famous "Pyramid of Success," where he breaks down the elements he believes are essential to success. He mentioned a verse of profoundly succinct poetry that inspired him to come up with this definition of success.

At God's footstool to confess
A poor soul knelt and bowed his head
"I failed" he cried
The Master said, "Thou didst thy best
That is success."

CHAPTER TWO

CHILDHOOD HEROES

My sports addiction began early. As a kid, I spent countless hours on hot summer days on the basketball court—dribbling, shooting, and rebounding against an imaginary opposition, trying to improve my game. I drove past Magic, dunked on Kareem, and shot over Bird. Winter afternoons were played out on a cold concrete surface in the schoolyard, where my friends and I would play five-on-five touch football games for hours. I caught impossible, Super Bowl–winning touchdowns from Montana, Marino, and Elway. I intercepted Theisman and tackled Riggins.

South Philadelphia is similar to other East Coast cities like New York or Boston. In our neighborhood, my friends and I played sports in the streets and in the local gyms. We were influenced by the athletes and teams we watched on TV, and also by many of the "Old Heads" in the neighborhood. These were guys a few years older, and many of them were brothers, cousins, and uncles of mine or my friends. They looked out for us and passed along their street wisdom to the next generation, and a couple of them even coached our teams in various leagues and tournaments over the years.

I still remember my elementary school basketball coach, Bobby "Cheech" DiFlorio, teaching us the "Triple Threat" position in basketball: When you first catch the ball, you keep your pivot foot set and just hold the ball. This way you have three options: You can dribble, pass, or shoot. The simple concept keeps a young player under control and puts a little thought behind his actions on the court. Details like that stick with you for a lifetime.

In interviewing such a diverse group of coaches, I hoped that asking them about their childhood heroes would show what they were like as kids and open up some of the same kinds of memories from their youth. When asked this question, about half of the coaches immediately said their parents were the most important influence in their young lives. Most of the rest referred to an athlete or athletes from their own generation.

It was really neat to hear the coaches view themselves as kids again and hear the respect and love that they still have for their parents. Angelo Dundee, for instance, who is in his seventies, still got choked up when he mentioned his father, calling him "Pop." Anne Donovan's voice was strong and resolute when she spoke about her mother, a single parent who raised eight children on her own.

We are all someone's little boy or girl, and it was nice to get in touch with that element of these revered coaches. When Marvin Lewis spoke of admiring Roberto Clemente for his ability to do everything on a baseball field, I could still hear the wonder and awe of a little boy. And Bill Parcells simply lit up when he recalled watching Willie Mays as a ten-year-old in New York.

People need heroes. No matter how successful a person becomes, there are people to look up to. I was lucky enough to interview many of my heroes in this book. Now they can tell you who their heroes were.

Who was your childhood hero and why?

RED AUERBACH

"Well, I grew up during the Depression and things were pretty tough—it was very difficult to have a hero per se, like they have today, you know what I mean? I always had a lot of awe and admiration for Lou Gehrig and Babe Ruth. But I think I saw them play one time in my life, because who had the money to go up there in those days to see them? But we'd read about them and talk about them. In those days we just didn't have the money to go see football or baseball."

Mr. Auerbach went on to acknowledge that he admired his father for his outgoing personality . . .

"Well, I admired my father, because although he was struggling, he was a guy who everybody liked. He was outgoing. I personally have never really been outgoing, you know what I mean? But I admired that in him. Wherever he went, he had friends right away. And he had a lot of common sense. I admired him, I really did."

Mr. Auerbach's father, Hyman, left Russia and moved to America when he was thirteen. He was a hardworking immigrant who, along with his American-born wife, Marie, owned a delicatessen in Brooklyn, New York.

DUSTY BAKER

"I had a couple of them. My football heroes were Jim Brown and Gale Sayers. For basketball it was Elgin Baylor, for track it was Bob Hayes, and for baseball it was Tommy Davis."

In his prime, Gale Sayers was one of the most talented running backs the NFL has ever seen . . .

CK: "Was there ever a better running back than Gale Sayers?"
DB: "I love Jim Brown but I was built more like Gale Sayers, you know what I mean?"
CK: "That guy was just amazing."

DB: "Yeah, when I played football I tried to emulate him. Tried to copy his cutback style and everything."

Elgin Baylor was a Hall of Fame forward for the Los Angeles Lakers; Bob Hayes was a gold medal–winning track star who was known as "the world's fastest human." He later became a standout wide receiver for the Dallas Cowboys. Tommy Davis was a star outfielder for the Los Angeles Dodgers who won batting titles in 1962 and 1963.

BRIAN BILLICK

"Gosh, there's so many. Not to sound too clichéd or emotional, but I think my parents were. My father had this incredible work ethic and my mother had a great deal of desire and ambition. And between the two of them, I think I fortunately inherited the best of both."

Both of Coach Billick's parents were born during the Great Depression and developed strong work ethics that were passed along to their son. His father, Don, was an air force pilot who often spent weeks away from the family home. He built every home in which the Billicks lived and Brian assisted him. His mother, Mildred, was a self-employed real estate agent who raised five children.

NICK BOLLETTIERI

"I really didn't have a childhood hero until my dad passed away. Then I realized what he said to me.

"When I dropped out of law school he said, 'Son, I'll support you in anything that you do, but you're responsible for all the results.' That gave me the courage to take risks and to try new things, because I knew I had my dad's blessing. Those words gave me the courage and the spirit to be curious about life—not just do the things that I thought I could do, but to be curious about things that only a few people think they can do."

Mr. Bollettieri's curiosity has compelled him to try new things, most specifically the Bollettieri Tennis Academy in Bradenton, Florida. The world-famous complex attracts players from all ages and walks of life to live and train for tennis there. It has produced world champions Andre Agassi, Jim Courier, and Monica Seles, to name a few.

BOBBY BOWDEN

"It was a guy named Jimmy Tarrant. I still communicate with him today; he's eighty-something years of age. But when I was about eight or nine years old, my dad was a Sunday school teacher down at my church, and one of his boys in his class was Jimmy Tarrant. He happened to be the star player on the Woodlawn High School football team. And my daddy would take me to the ball games when I was eight, nine, and ten to watch Woodlawn High School and Jimmy Tarrant. No doubt in my mind he was my first boyhood hero."

Bobby Bowden, inspired by his hero, Jimmy Tarrant, went on to become the star quarterback at Woodlawn High School himself. It was in these early days as a young quarterback that Bowden received formative training in game strategy and team leadership, laying the foundation of gridiron knowledge that would help him become one of college football's greatest coaches.

SCOTTY BOWMAN

"It was a player in Boston named Bill Cowley. The games were on the radio when I was living in Montreal as a kid. We used to get the Boston games in clear and I used to follow them, and I just happened to like the way Cowley sounded. Besides, he was a great centerman and, in fact, a playmaker. I got to meet him later because he owned a junior team.

"The reason I followed him is because Boston was my team then. I was impressed with him and at the time they said, 'He makes more wings, meaning wingers, than Boeing.' I got a kick out of that.

"They had another centerman, Milt Schmidt, who was probably the best they had, but I just happened to gravitate to Cowley. That's a long time ago, probably sixty-five years. He was my hero at the time. Bill Cowley. My parents got me a jersey with his number on it, number ten."

Mr. Bowman got a chance to meet his boyhood idol when he became a coach . . .

CK: "Did you get a chance to tell him that he was your hero as a youngster?"

SB: "Yes, my first job in 1956 was in Ottawa, and I met him there. He later owned a part of the junior team, the Ottawa 67s, but I met him before he owned the team. It was kinda neat to meet a guy many years later, you know."

Bill Cowley was a star centerman for the Boston Bruins in the 1930s and 1940s. He was known as an outstanding playmaker for his ability to pass the puck "on a dime" to his wingmen. Cowley won the Hart Trophy as MVP of the league in 1941 and 1943.

JOHN CHANEY

"My childhood hero was a man by the name of Sam Brown. He was my everything, like a father to me, since I don't know who my real father is. Sam Brown was my basketball coach at Ben Franklin High School when I played there. He was a Jewish guy that looked after us in south Philadelphia, and all the players around the city during that time. He was just the most meaningful person to me; he taught me so much about what was important.

"In those days Sam Brown was the only person that convinced me that I *had* to go to college. He also convinced my mom and my pop that I *had* to go to college. I had a stepfather at the time, and he and my mom expected me to go get a nine-to-five job.

"In the summer he would take us up to Camp Stony Hollow in the Poconos. We'd stay there all summer. He'd go out and get us clothing and he looked out for us. Tried to find a job for us during the summertime. He did the things that helped make me what I am today. I attribute all of that to him."

Inspired by Sam Brown, Coach Chaney graduated from Bethune-Cookman College in 1955 and has been a basketball coach for five decades. He has run his own summer basketball camp for the past twenty-five years.

BILL COWHER

"I don't know if I ever had one hero. I think I looked up to a lot of different football players because of how they played: Jack Lambert, Dick Butkus, Ray Nitschke. I did love to play the game of football, and I loved how they played it. The biggest thing I loved about it is they played the game with passion; they had a purpose on the field. I know that was something I tried to bring on the field every time I played."

Jack Lambert was the heart of the Pittsburgh Steelers' Steel Curtain defense, which won four Super Bowls in the 1970s. Dick Butkus was the legendary Chicago Bears linebacker who is considered by many to be the greatest linebacker to ever play professional football. And Ray Nitchske was the middle linebacker on Vince Lombardi's Green Bay Packers dynasty of the 1960s. All three are in the NFL Hall of Fame.

Anyone who has seen Coach Cowher on the sidelines knows he coaches with the same ferocious passion and intensity with which Lambert, Butkus, and Nitschke played.

ANNE DONOVAN

"Definitely my mother. I was five years old when my father passed away and I was the youngest of eight children. To watch her raise eight successful, confident, intelligent, working children was very powerful for me to see. It wasn't something she preached or that she told us she was doing for us, it was just that she recognized when my father passed that she had to step to the plate and she now had the responsibility of eight children to raise on her own. I think unconsciously that had a huge impact on me."

Coach Donovan's father died of a heart ailment when she was five years old. Her mother took over running the house while working at a women's center and collecting social security. Six of her eight children received athletic scholarships to college.

ANGELO DUNDEE

"My father, because of the way he showed his strength and the ability to handle all the kids. And my daddy couldn't read or write—couldn't speak English, just Italian. He was my hero because he did so much with each of us. There were nine of us. Pop raised the family, while buying three or four houses with the twenty-four bucks a week he used to make. And you know, it wasn't like today with the luxuries of the world, like television. I looked up to my father."

Dundee is a first-generation Italian American. His parents instilled in their son the honest, family-oriented qualities for which he became known. He established himself as a man of integrity in a sport often devoid of such qualities.

TONY DUNGY

"I looked up to a lot of sports figures; I was always interested in athletics. But as a child growing up, I'd have to say Martin Luther King. It was that time in our country—the 1960s. Dr. King had a unique way of making people really feel strongly about what was right and what was wrong. I admired that. I was at a very impressionable age at that time, and I just thought he was right on in terms of trying to make this country as great as it can be. Trying to lift everyone to have that same ideal and same goal. I just thought he was fantastic."

Civil rights leader Martin Luther King Jr. had an enormous impact on an entire generation of young Americans, and his views and nonviolent approach made him stand out as a voice of conscience in the turbulent 1960s. His "I Have a Dream" speech is among the most stirring in American history. Dr. King was tragically gunned down by an assassin in 1968. Coach Dungy's inner strength evokes Dr. King's leadership qualities.

HERMAN EDWARDS

"When I was younger, it was Jim Thorpe. I actually watched the movie on TV, watched Burt Lancaster play him. I watched what he had to go through in his life, the ups and downs, and for the most part I always believed that success comes to people who habitually do things that unsuccessful people don't attempt to do. And it seemed to me that he was that type of guy. He had the mental fortitude to just keep doing things that other people wouldn't even attempt to do. He knew what his talent was early in life. He figured out what that was and used his ability. That's one thing I understood as a young guy, when you look at guys, I believe God gives everyone a talent, but a lot of people never find out what their talent is. They want to do this, that. And for me, watching that as a young guy, I wanted to be like him. I wanted to be an athlete.

"And the next guy, because I grew up in the civil rights era, was Muhammad Ali. The thing I liked about him the most was that he took a stand and was willing to give up what he accomplished. When he was the heavyweight champion of the world, whether it was right, wrong, or indifferent, he wasn't going to join the service. He took a big hit on that. He was willing to give up his career, and that made me look up and go, 'Wow!' With everything this guy has accomplished and what he's really saying is, 'I really believe this, and I'm willing to give all of this up.' That to me was the key.

"Those were the two guys that I looked up to and admired when I was growing up."

Jim Thorpe (1888–1953) won the pentathlon and decathlon at the 1912 Olympic games in Stockholm, and played professional baseball and football. Sweden's King Gustav V called Thorpe "the greatest athlete in the world."

Muhammad Ali is one of the world's most well-known athletes. In 1967 he was stripped of the heavyweight championship for his refusal to join the army during the Vietnam War. He later became the first man to win the world heavyweight championship three times.

JEFF FISHER

"My father. He was there, he was the one I looked up to. He was the one that disciplined us and motivated us and explained what we did not understand. He was the one that identified athletes as sports heroes, or those individuals that you should look up to. And those perhaps that you shouldn't.

"I believe the hero that we look up to should always be one that is giving us the right direction."

DAN GABLE

"Well, I grew up in a YMCA. From the ages of four to twelve, I was there on a daily basis. I remember those people, and it was forty years ago. Chuck Hazama, Wally Lessman—these people were very influential to me. It was the people in that YMCA, the Young Men's Christian Association, that really gave me a day-in, day-out basis for developing an attitude for competition, for sportsmanship, for daily living.

"Along with that I was sports-crazy on all levels, and Mickey Mantle was probably the biggest name that I tried to emulate, even though later on we found out that he had some character flaws. But he came forth, and by the time he passed on, there were no problems."

"The Mick," Mickey Mantle, was a legendary center fielder for the New York Yankees in the 1950s and 1960s. His country-boy humbleness and boyish charms made him an instant favorite across the nation. His unique combination of speed and power from both sides of the plate made him the greatest power-hitting switch-hitter in baseball history. He led the Yankees to twelve World Series appearances.

Later in his life, Mantle admitted to being an alcoholic and, in fact, received a liver transplant prior to his death in 1995. However, he became a strong advocate against drinking before he died.

BRAD GILBERT

"As a kid I used to love Rick Barry—he used to play for the Warriors. What a great basketball player he was. I just loved his grit and I just remember how teared up I got when the Warriors won the championship in 1975. And a fictional character I just loved was James Bond. He was so cool."

A northern California native, Mr. Gilbert was a Golden State Warriors fan. Hall of Famer Rick Barry led the Warriors to the NBA title in 1975. Barry was known for his aggressive competitiveness and his remarkably accurate underhanded free-throw style. Barry had an 89.3 lifetime free-throw percentage, the second highest in NBA history.

When further pressed to choose a favorite Bond actor, Gilbert says it's a tough call between Roger Moore and Sean Connery.

CARRIE GRAF

"I guess I had a lot of them, but they're Australian-rules football players. Because as a young female growing up in Australia there weren't a lot of high-priced female athletes. So I modeled myself on Australian-rules football stars. They were who I wanted to be when I played around on the street."

Australian-rules football is one of the hardest-hitting and fastest-moving games in the world. Played between two teams of eighteen players on an oval field, it is similar to American football, but is distinguished by the relatively free movement of the ball (partly due to the absence of an offside rule), and the fact that the players wear no pads. It is the most popular winter sport in Australia.

APRIL HEINRICHS

"Unequivocally my father. That's probably not a unique answer. My father, Melvin Heinrichs, is not my real father—I've never actually met my real father. Melvin met my mother and they got married at about the time a child becomes capable of remembering things, capable of talking and communicating. We hit it off and from that day forth it was really as if he was my biological father anyway.

"I'm sure that the reason we hit it off is because I was drawn to athletics and he was a good athlete; we had that connection. His work ethic was very strong; he was a good person. He was a fireman. And I remember when they were dating (or they may have been just married at this point) and people would come up to me and say, 'Oh, we just love Melvin, he's so sweet.' 'Oh, I just love that Melvin, you're so lucky to have him.' Everybody kept telling me how great he was.

"So between that and the sports connection, I quickly learned that he was such a great guy. Everywhere he went, I went. He toted me around on his motorcycle. I rode in the fire truck. I went to work. I raced home to tell him about soccer practice or basketball or track. We had that connection."

Coach Heinrichs's stepfather, Melvin, was a Denver, Colorado, firefighter who became the guiding influence in her life, so much so that she legally changed her last name to his. She was so connected to him that when her mother and Melvin divorced during her freshman year of high school, she chose to live with her stepfather, stating, "There was never any doubt where I'd go."

WHITEY HERZOG

"I would think that from the time I was seven or eight years old I was into baseball—all sports, pretty much—and growing up in St. Louis, I'd have to say it was Stan Musial. And even to this day (he's eighty-one or eighty-two now); he's become a very good friend. He's a great person, not only a Hall of Fame baseball player, but a Hall of Fame person. I always tell him he ruined my career, because the first time I ever saw him play, he hit four doubles and I tried to copy his stance—and that's it, I was never any good anymore."

Stan "the Man" Musial is a baseball legend. During his Hall of Fame career he won seven National League batting titles, was named to twenty all-star teams, and was MVP of the National League in 1943, 1946, and 1948. He played his entire career with the St. Louis Cardinals.

KEN HITCHCOCK

"I have two of them: my father, who died at a very young age, when I was fourteen and he was forty, and Gordie Howe, who remains my hero to this day. Gordie Howe to me was the ultimate athlete. He was a player that had longevity, class, dignity, charisma. He had everything. He was a person that my father gravitated to and I followed my father that way."

Known as "Mr. Hockey," Gordie Howe won four Stanley Cups, took league MVP six times, and was a twenty-one-time all-star during his Hall of Fame career. He is considered by many to be the greatest all-around player in hockey history.

BELA KAROLYI

"I don't really remember a childhood hero, but definitely in my teenage years it was my mentor and coach, George Comonaru. He was my physical education professor. He was also the dean of the university, a man who stands out from most of the people I have ever known with his character, his integrity. He was my hero in many different ways, and at the same time, he was my idol."

As a student attending a physical education college in Romania, Karolyi cut classes to participate in various sports. The dean confronted him, and advised him to focus on one thing—pursuing a career as a teacher, not as an athlete. Coach Karolyi listened and devoted himself full-time to his studies, and graduated second in his class (his wife, Marta, was first). This decision changed Karolyi's life and altered the course of women's gymnastics history.

TRUDI LACEY

"I had two of them, actually. One was—believe it or not—Lew Alcindor, who later became Kareem Abdul Jabbar. I read a book on him, about how he grew up in New York, and went on to get a college scholarship at UCLA, and then became a great professional player. And Walt Frazier. Defensively he did great things, and I always thought defensive players got overlooked. So I kind of liked Kareem's emergence from New York to play for a great coach—I love John Wooden. And I followed the Knicks a lot back then and their great teams, and Frazier stood out because of his defense."

Coach Lacey identified with two of the Big Apple's most famous basketball products. Kareem Abdul Jabbar was a high school phenom who attended Power Memorial High School and went on to become a colle-

giate and professional great, winning three national college titles while attending UCLA, and then six NBA championships, one with the Milwaukee Bucks and five with the Los Angeles Lakers.

Walt "Clyde" Frazier was the point guard for the New York Knicks of the late 1960s and early 1970s. He led the Knicks to two NBA championships and was named to the NBA's All-Defensive Team seven times. He was elected to the NBA Hall of Fame in 1987. Frazier was nicknamed Clyde after Clyde Barrow, of Bonnie and Clyde, for his proficiency at stealing the basketball from opponents.

MARVIN LEWIS

"Roberto Clemente, for the way he played baseball. Hitting, running, fielding, throwing—he did it all."

Roberto Clemente is a beloved figure in his native Puerto Rico and one of baseball's all-time greats. The Pittsburgh Pirates right fielder won twelve Gold Gloves and was an eleven-time all-star. He was named league MVP in 1966 and won four National League batting titles. Clemente led the league in outfield assists five times, and won two World Series, in 1960 and 1971—he had a hit in every game of each series—and was named MVP of the 1971 World Series.

On New Year's Eve 1972, Clemente was tragically killed in an airplane crash while attempting to deliver supplies to earthquake victims in Nicaragua.

LUTE OLSON

"Well, I lost my father when I was five, and I had a brother who was about five years older than me—and he was somebody that I really respected. He sort of took over the role as the adviser even though he was very young. He was a very good athlete and was very active in a lot of different things. I looked up to him and everything that he accomplished. He was the person that I was trying to compete with.

"And beyond him it was always my coaches. When I got to the high school and college levels, the coaches really had more of an effect than anybody."

After Olson's father died of a massive stroke, his brother and coaches nurtured the youngster's athletic abilities. He became a three-sport star (basketball, baseball, and football) in high school and college, and earned a ticket out of the close-knit North Dakota community where he grew up.

TOM OSBORNE

"Well, I think probably my dad in many respects. He was in World War II, so he was gone from about the age of five until I was about ten. He was overseas much of that time and I didn't know him very well, but I really looked up to him and admired him.

"And probably athletically speaking, when I was junior high school age and really prone to hero worship, a guy named Bobby Reynolds. He played football at the University of Nebraska. He was from Grand Island, Nebraska, which was twenty-two miles from Hastings, my hometown. He was a great high school athlete, and then he was an All-American halfback at the University of Nebraska."

Bobby Reynolds was one of the greatest athletes in Nebraska state history. He excelled in football and basketball, leading his high school football team in 1947 and 1948 to unbeaten seasons and state championships. In basketball, teams he played on won two state championships and had a 44–1 record. He was also a standout in track.

BILL PARCELLS

"When I was young, baseball was the preeminent sport at the time, along with horse racing and boxing. Football and basketball were not primary sports when I was a ten-year-old. So I would have to say, being in the New York area, that Willie Mays was the guy that I thought about the most, that I saw and witnessed. He was a young player coming up right there in the early fifties. You know, I was about ten years old. He was my guy. He was the best player I ever saw."

Known as the "Say Hey Kid," Willie Mays played with an energetic enthusiasm that made him one of the most exciting and popular players in the game. His statistics rank with the all-time greats, finishing fourth all-time in home runs (660), and third in total bases (6,066). He was named league MVP in 1954 and 1965 and played in twenty all-star games.

MIKE SCIOSCIA

"You know, at the time, growing up I came from a very tight, close-knit family. And my upbringing was very sports-oriented. I remember watching baseball—I really idolized Johnny Bench, and Thurman Munson, too. I was drawn to those two guys.

"But if you ask me who my real hero and role model was, looking back, there were two of them: my dad and my older brother. I think that's something that, as time passes and you reflect on it, you realize how much you bonded with them, and how close you were with them, as opposed to what you think is important at that time."

As catcher on the "Big Red Machine," Johnny Bench was the cornerstone of the Cincinnati Reds' two World Series championship teams of the 1970s. A complete player, Bench was a feared hitter, and won ten Gold Gloves for his ability to both handle pitchers and throw out runners on the base paths. He was named league MVP in 1970 and 1972 and was elected to the Hall of Fame in 1989.

Catcher Thurman Munson was the captain of the New York Yankees' 1977 and 1978 world championship teams. He was American League Rookie of the Year in 1970, won Gold Gloves in 1973, 1974, and 1975, and was a seven-time all-star.

Thurman Munson's life was sadly cut short when the two-engine Cessna he was piloting crashed on August 2, 1979. To this day, Thurman Munson's jersey still hangs in his empty locker as a tribute to the Yankees' fallen captain.

TUBBY SMITH

"Growing up it was probably my older brother. He was ten years older than me, and I really looked up to him because of his athleticism. Talking about other folks I looked up to, I liked Oscar Robertson.

"But growing up on a farm, I didn't really have a lot of them. I wasn't really exposed to professional sports until much later when my dad used to drive a school bus, and I finally got a chance to go see the Baltimore Orioles, the Baltimore Bullets, and the Washington Senators."

Oscar Robertson, "The Big O," was a six-foot-five, 220-pound basket-ball player who revolutionized the point guard position in the NBA. Robertson could score and rebound, as well as pass. Remarkably, in the 1961–62 season, he averaged a triple-double with 30.8 points, 11.4 assists, and 12.5 rebounds per game, a feat that has never been dupli-cated. In 1971, he led the Milwaukee Bucks to their first and only world championship.

EMANUEL STEWARD

"I was into boxing all the time, so the guy that I liked the most was Floyd Patterson. At the time, I'd say he was my boxing hero. And Sugar Ray Robinson.

"As I got older, the greatest champion and the greatest human being I've known was Joe Louis. He was a phenomenal man, even though at the time I didn't pay that much attention. But his accomplishments, what he did for racial relationships, what he did for the country, the image that he kept—there has never been a man to me that had the word 'champion' so stamped on him the way this man did.

"And the fight between him and Max Schmeling is the greatest single event to me in the history of the world. That night the whole world was on edge, because the fight was taking the direction that the war and the whole world was moving in, confined into a little ring. It was a man from Germany and a man from America—he was not a black man that night, he was an American that night to the whole world. And for Joe Louis to come out and knock Schmeling out in such dramatic fashion, especially when you know that Schmeling had knocked him out before—the whole world erupted, people just celebrating. Those are the things that make no one able to beat Joe Louis in my mind. You see what I mean? It's because of the emotions. I think Ali would have beaten him in the ring, but that's boxing. Joe Louis embodies the word 'champion' to me. A fine human being."

On June 22, 1938, with America nearing involvement in World War II, Joe Louis, an African American, met Max Schmeling, a German, for the heavyweight boxing championship of the world.

The fight was held in a sold-out Yankee Stadium and broadcast to millions more on radio. Adolf Hitler listened to a live feed of the fight in Germany. Moments after the opening bell, Louis hit Schmeling with a short, overhand right, buckling the German's knees. Louis then unleashed a barrage of punches, paralyzing Schmeling and sending him to the canvas twice before his corner threw in the towel.

Louis obliterated Hitler's superrace theory and ignited national pride among all Americans. He went on to become one of the greatest heavyweight champions in history. Schmeling would never again challenge for the title.

JOE TORRE

"I always look to my brother Frank. I had an older brother, Rocco, but when I was ten or eleven years old he got married, and he wasn't really a part of our household, even though we were a close-knit family.

"Frank sort of took over after my father left, because he and my mom split when I was about twelve or thirteen. And actually, my brother Frank was responsible for asking him to leave, because he was abusive to my mom. So Frank has been pretty much the one that I needed validation from. He took on that role. He put me through high school; I went to a private high school and he paid my way. And I used to go visit him when I was a teenager and he was playing in the minor leagues in different places. So he was the one who was always my hero. I needed the validation from him, and it wasn't easy. I hated him for a time, especially when I was a teenager and in my early time in baseball because he was very critical of me. It was a long time before I felt that I had gained his approval."

Frank Torre was known for his fielding, leading National League first basemen in fielding in 1957 and 1958. On September 2, 1957, he tied a National League mark by scoring six runs in one game, and then hit two home runs in the World Series to help the Braves beat the Yankees.

JOHN TORTORELLA

"There's no one specific childhood hero. I guess when you're growing up, your parents are always the people you're looking to and I guess they have to be—as far as development—the people you look at. Other than that, there's no one specific childhood hero. When I was growing up I was a big fan of Derek Sanderson. He was the kind of guy that I always liked watching. But a hero? I don't think there's any one particular hero; you're looking for all bits and pieces from people that you think will develop you."

Derek Sanderson was a tough center for the Boston Bruins in the late 1960s and 1970s. He helped Boston win two Stanley Cups (1969–70 and 1971–72). He was a popular player with a rebel image, sporting long hair and a mustache.

DICK VERMEIL

"I'd have to say my dad. And I'm not sure it was looked upon as a hero at the time. There was more of a respectful fear factor there."

Coach Vermeil's father, Louis, was a perfectionist and workaholic auto mechanic who would occasionally work twenty-four consecutive hours just because he could do it. Dick emulates much of his father's work ethic, but interestingly differs from him in the important fact that while

Vermeil's father was quick to criticize his son, Coach Vermeil heaps praise upon those he coaches.

BILL WALSH

"My childhood heroes were the players on the USC football team. I lived about a mile from the school, so I'd walk or take the streetcar down, hang out at the practices, and play catch with the guys. They were receptive and that really nurtured my interest in football. So my heroes were the players of the USC teams of the late 1940s and early 1950s."

The University of Southern California has one of the richest football traditions in the nation. Since 1922 they have won twenty-nine bowl games, including two consecutive national championships, in 2003 and 2004. Among their most outstanding players are Ronnie Lott, Marcus Allen, and Reggie Bush.

LENNY WILKENS

"There were two people. One was a priest friend in our parish, a guy named Tom Mannion. He was like a big brother. My dad died when I was five, and Tom was a guy who was always around the school. I went to Holy Rosary Catholic Elementary School. And he was always there encouraging us as young people. I got to know him because I served Mass; I was an altar boy. He reinforced the values my mom taught us and it seemed that he was always telling me, 'You can accomplish it. You can do this, you can do that.' He always had a positive swing on things and he kept telling me that the only one who would stop me would be me. It was nice to hear that from somebody.

It was always a positive thing that you can be successful, but you're the one that has to do the work.

"The other one was Jackie Robinson. I grew up in Brooklyn, and of course the Dodgers were everything in that era. And I remember when he came to the team, being the first African American, and the thing that stood out to me about this guy's character was that I never saw any quit in him, he never made excuses for himself, he came to play every game, and whatever was necessary, he did it. And he went through a lot. I know some of the catcalls that were made at him and things like that. And yet, he never made an excuse for himself. And I thought, wow, this is a man."

In 1947 Jackie Robinson shattered baseball's color barrier by becoming the first African American to play in Major League Baseball. Robinson was picked by Dodgers president Branch Rickey as the first black player not only for his abundant playing ability, but also for his resilience as a person. Robinson's strength of character allowed him to overcome the widespread ignorance and overt racism that were prevalent in the United States in the late 1940s and 1950s.

Robinson made an immediate impact at second base, winning Rookie of the Year in 1947. In 1949 he won National League MVP and the batting title with a .342 average. He was elected to the Hall of Fame in 1962.

JOHN WOODEN

"My father. He was a good man who never had an unkind word to say about anyone. He tried to teach me and my brothers that you should never try to be better than anyone else, but never cease trying to be the best you could be, and always learn from others."

Joshua Wooden, Coach Wooden's father, gave his son the following seven-point creed, upon which Coach Wooden later built his own Pyramid for Success:

> *Be true to yourself.*
> *Make each day your masterpiece.*
> *Help others.*
> *Drink deeply from good books.*
> *Make friendship a fine art.*
> *Build shelter against a rainy day.*
> *Pray for guidance and give thanks for your blessings every day.*

CHAPTER THREE

THE BEST ADVICE

Don't give up, don't ever give up.

I was a curious kid, always asking questions, pestering adults and teachers for answers to things I hadn't yet experienced. Such inquisitiveness is an excellent quality for a youngster (unless you're the one answering the questions), because curiosity leads to creativity and excitement about life.

My main interest was sports, so I wanted to know who was the best player, the best coach, the best team—from Don Shula's "perfect" Miami Dolphins to the volatile Billy Martin and his tempestuous New York Yankees. As I got older and my interests expanded, I tried to familiarize myself with whoever was at the top in the entertainment and business worlds. I was always observing the best of whichever profession I was focused on at the time.

I knew that whoever was the best at the moment had not always been the best. They had started out like me, a kid, and become the best. How did they get there? Who taught them? Did they have secrets that would help me? Whatever advice they had gotten had worked, and if I could get some of that knowledge, maybe I could become the best at something (I'm still trying). That's how this question (and ultimately, this book) came about.

The coaches here give advice for a living, and they are the best at it. What tips had they received on their way to the top that helped them the most? Ralph Waldo Emerson once said, "Common sense is genius dressed in its working clothes." Surprisingly, many of the coaches were given simple, commonsense advice that left such an impression it's lasted a lifetime. For example, Brad Gilbert's coach telling him to "never be late for anything, ever" or Bill Parcells's father telling him to "first decide what he wants, then have the staying power to achieve it," the advice they received developed the work ethic that has produced many of the greatest winners in the history of American sports.

Another recurring answer was to believe in themselves and in what they were doing. Once they had that first building block, the rest would become possible.

When I thought about the best advice I ever got, one voice kept coming back to me. In 1992, former North Carolina State basketball coach Jim Valvano was dying of lung cancer. He was giving a speech at the first ever ESPY awards, when he implored the audience with words I had heard before, but never with the conviction of a man facing death. Jimmy V said, "Don't give up, don't ever give up!"

What is the best advice you were ever given?

RED AUERBACH

"[Laughs.] Well, a lot of people gave me advice. But I remember the first bit of advice that was really significant was from my high school physical education teacher. He grabbed me up against the wall one time and he said, 'Don't you for one minute think because you play a little basketball that it's gonna carry you for the rest of your life. You better really hit those books and become a man.' And I never forgot that. A guy by the name of Alvin Borten."

Auerbach earned his bachelor's and master's degrees in physical education at George Washington University, graduating in 1940. Then in order to gain experience, he taught history and coached basketball and baseball at the high school level before moving on to coach professional basketball.

DUSTY BAKER

"As far as managing, Roger Craig told me to try to put people in situations that they're most likely to succeed in. And to try to learn your personnel as well as the opposition's."

Roger Craig is the former manager of the San Francisco Giants and San Diego Padres. He is well known as a teacher of the split-fingered fastball to pitchers such as Mike Scott and Jack Morris. He led the Giants to the NL West title in 1987 and the pennant in 1989. Dusty Baker replaced Craig as manager of the Giants in 1992.

BRIAN BILLICK

"It's probably clichéd, but you've got to stay true to yourself. We've all been influenced by people in our careers, but particularly when you become a head coach, I think that people too often try to emulate someone specifically that maybe is not true to their character. And that inevitably is going to fail you because you're not able to maintain a consistent level of interaction when it's not true to your demeanor."

CK: "That's true, it takes time for you to become comfortable with yourself."

BB: "Right, and in a crisis situation, which is when it becomes most apparent, if you're constantly trying to be somebody else, you will hesitate, you will be unsure, because at some point in every job, instincts have to kick in. And you have to stay true to your inherent beliefs because if you're constantly just copying somebody, so to speak, then in a crisis situation you're gonna be lost."

Before becoming a head coach, Billick was a member of former Min-nesota Vikings' coach Denny Green's staff for almost ten years (1989–98), and though he often cites Green and Bill Walsh as his men-tors, Billick is clearly his own man.

NICK BOLLETTIERI

"The most important advice that I've heard over the last fifty years is to believe in myself. There's no stronger thing in life than knowing who you are, and that you believe you can do things. There's no self-doubt. That's the strongest thing, to believe in yourself."

Bollettieri has the confident swagger and thick accent of his native New York. His individuality and strong persona let people know imme-diately that he believes in himself.

BOBBY BOWDEN

"My dad gave me some good advice. He told me one time, 'Bobby, don't forget as you go through life, that you're as good as anybody.'

"And if you want to know what significance that had . . . I had a tendency to feel inferior, to feel I couldn't do some of the things I wanted to do, and he was just trying to tell me I could. And as I went through life, I found it to be true."

CK: "So he gave you some confidence."

BB: "I think so. And I always wondered where he got that advice, and I think back to when he came up. It was during the Depression, and he had no daddy. They said he was selling newspapers on the corner when he was about ten. And he probably went through a life not knowing if he was ever going to make it. Not thinking he was good enough and stuff like that, you know? And I've always appreciated his advice."

CK: "It's a great gift he gave you."

BB: "It is."

Coach Bowden has taken his father's advice and today he is a father figure to many of his players, often standing by them in the face of harsh criticism. He is affectionately known to Seminole fans as the "Papa 'Nole."

SCOTTY BOWMAN

"A person has to be his own guy. You can take good ideas from a lot of people, but you also have to have some of your own. You've got to be creative, you've got to have your own ideas."

Bowman blended traditional hockey coaching with new innovations, studying video and using computers for statistical information before other coaches did. He became known as a brilliant strategist with an almost photographic memory of other teams' players and game plans.

JOHN CHANEY

"I think one of the things for me—having come out of the teaching profession where I taught both high school and college, classes like the psychology of sports and so forth—one of the most important things is trying to discern the difference between meaning and effect. Knowing that both can be very elusive, the meaning of what you do and the effect of what you do.

"A dear friend of mine, Al McGuire, one of our great coaches who has passed away, said that the word *no* is a good answer. [Laughs.] Don't be afraid to use the word *no*. It's a good answer. [Laughing.] No, I don't know. No, I didn't see; no, I didn't hear; no, I don't understand."

Al McGuire was a Hall of Fame college basketball coach who led Marquette University to the national championship in 1977. McGuire passed away in 2001.

BILL COWHER

"I would say to never take yourself too seriously, particularly if you've had success. What makes you realize that is that it takes more than one person to make your success—that's an element of being a part of a team."

For all his burning intensity, Coach Cowher has tapped into a lighter side of himself in recent years. He has become a media favorite, appearing frequently to offer commentary and appear in television ads.

ANNE DONOVAN

"There's no substitute for hard work. You can overcome lack of talent and good fortune with how hard you work. That was something my mother instilled in us as children and has always stayed with me. It was a strength of mine as a player and is really a strength of mine now as a coach."

Coach Donovan picked up her work ethic from her mother and carried it onto the court as a player—where she became known as a tireless worker—and also to the teams she's coached, which employ a relentless defensive style and try to outwork their opponents.

ANGELO DUNDEE

"The best advice I ever got was from a fella named Steve Ellis. He was an announcer and friend. He told me one thing, he said, 'Ange, whenever you get into a conversation with people and they ask you a question, don't just spout out what you have in mind; digest it for a while, then come out with a statement. This way you can give a better evaluation of what they're asking.' And I listened to that."

Dundee needed to be a good listener, working with one of sports' greatest talkers, Muhammad Ali.

TONY DUNGY

"I've gotten a lot of good advice over the years, but I think probably the best advice I got was from my dad, when he always told me to not complain about problems and look for solutions. I've found that over the years that's really a good way to approach things."

Coach Dungy was extremely close with his father, a college science professor, and after his dad passed away, Tony joined Family First, a nonprofit research and communication organization based in Tampa, Florida. He is a spokesman for their All-Pro Dad program. Through this program, he raises awareness about the importance of fatherhood through speeches, media interviews, and in public-service announcements on television.

HERMAN EDWARDS

"Probably it was from my dad, who said to choose your friends wisely and don't let them choose you. If you can understand that, you'll be OK."

Herman Edwards Sr., a longtime army sergeant, was a black American who met Herman's mother, a white German, shortly after World War II. After moving back to the United States, they encountered racism from both blacks and whites who did not accept their interracial marriage. Coach Edwards credits his father with teaching him many of the leadership qualities he is now known for. Herman Sr. passed away when Coach Edwards was twenty-four.

JEFF FISHER

"I remember a long time ago someone told me, 'Don't let anyone tell you that you're lucky, because luck is what happens at the intersection of preparation and opportunity.' If you're prepared and you're given an opportunity, most of the time you'll take advantage and be successful."

In the 2000 play-offs against the Buffalo Bills, preparation, opportunity, and a little luck came together for Tennessee. With three seconds remaining in the game and Buffalo ahead 16–15, Titan Frank Wychek received the Bills' kickoff and lateraled the ball across the field to teammate Kevin Dyson, who ran it seventy-five yards for a touchdown. The play became known as the "Music City Miracle," and it propelled the Titans to a Super Bowl appearance that year.

DAN GABLE

"That's a tough question to answer. The reason I say that is because one gets a lot of advice. But I'd say that *who* gives you the advice determines if you can put it in the category of *best* advice. So right away you are limited to people you respect or love or really care for, or that are very meaningful to you. And that's a category with only a few people because you know they're looking out for you.

"Of that mind I would probably say between my parents, who I think put the seed into my head, and then once it went beyond that to some good people that were influential in enforcing what my parents had given me, which is that you *listen and believe.* And when people are telling you good things because they're good people and they care about you, then it's very important that you are coachable. Listening and believing will give people an opportunity to do some enormous things.

"And beyond that, having the ability to put that advice into action is even more important.

"The first part—the listening and believing—came from my parents and carried on through my coaches. Then it was reinforced and put into action through a lot of these people I'm talking about. There was a book called *Heart of a Champion* by Bob Richards. I listened to his speech and then I bought one of his books. He was a pole vault champion back in 1952 in the Olympic games. And he was the first person ever on a Wheaties cereal box. He gave lots of advice in his book, but he said that when people get advice they just dream about stuff and they don't put things into action, which causes [the dreams to become] reality. Without action you'll have no gold medals."

Bob Richards is one of the greatest track and field athletes in U.S. history. He won gold medals in the pole vault at the 1952 and 1956 Olympic games, and claimed three U.S. decathlon championships, in 1951, 1954, and 1955. In 1957 he wrote The Heart of a Champion, *a hugely popular book among athletes and coaches.*

BRAD GILBERT

"My coach when I was eighteen, Tom Chivington, told me, 'Don't ever be late. Ever. If you're late, you're not respecting the rest of the guys on the team.' And I've never been late for anything the rest of my life."

Tom Chivington coached Brad Gilbert at Foothill College in Los Altos Hills, California, in the early 1980s. Under Chivington's guidance, the Foothill men's tennis program won twenty-six conference titles, twenty-one northern California championships, and thirteen state titles over thirty-four years. Chivington retired in 2001.

CARRIE GRAF

"One of the best pieces of advice I was given was if you want to be something, act like what that is. I heard one of my coaches and mentors say to an athlete, 'If you want to be an Olympian, act like an Olympian.' That really struck a chord with me. Often young people or young players say, 'Well, when I get to that place in the Olympics, I'll start working harder or training harder.' But the point is, if that's where you want to go, you need to start acting that way. And I think if you can act it, you can become it."

Coach Graf was an assistant coach with the Australian national team in 1996, when they won the Olympic bronze medal in Atlanta, and again in 2000, when they took the silver at the games in Sydney, Australia.

APRIL HEINRICHS

"One is to trust people until they give you a reason not to trust them. I think that's really a reflection of an optimistic and positive lifestyle.

Because if it's the other way around, then you're living a life of questioning and wondering and possibly having negative interpretations of communication.

"So I think truly the best advice, whether you're a soccer coach or a basketball coach or a person out in life is that: to trust people until they give you a reason not to."

April Heinrichs's upbringing wasn't traditional. She was born April Minnis in Denver, Colorado, but she never met her biological father, and her mother struggled with the family until she met the man who would become April's stepfather, Melvin Heinrichs.

KEN HITCHCOCK

"I got two pieces of advice. The best advice I ever got when I was looking to become a full-time coach (rather than an amateur coach or a volunteer coach) was if you think they want you as a coach and you want the job bad enough, make sure that you don't overprice yourself, because they've already interviewed about twenty other people. If you want to start, be prepared to start on the ground floor. Don't try to start on the twelfth floor.

"And the second best piece of advice I got was that your major concern as a coach is not what they're saying or thinking when you're in the room, it's what they're saying and thinking when you're out of the room."

Hitchcock's coaching career didn't start on the top floor; it began in 1984 with the Kamloops Blazers of the Western Hockey League. He led the Blazers to two WHL championship victories, in 1985–86 and 1989–90.

BELA KAROLYI

"It was from the dean of my university, George Comonaru. His advice was, 'Always be yourself. Don't try to copy anybody.' And of course at the time the communist regime tried to mold everybody in the same kind of way. You had to follow a particular line, so obviously you had to change your attitude and how you related with people. That was so impressive to me. Be yourself.

"I followed that advice in my coaching career and later I found out more and more how important it is for a person to believe that what you are doing is your own. It is not a copy of someone else, it's not a false copy, but it is yours. That gives you confidence. That gives you the belief that what you are doing is really up to you. And at the same time, when good or bad things happen, you are responsible."

In the early 1980s, after Karolyi and his wife, Marta, defected to the United States from communist Romania, a group of businessmen invested in the couple to open a gymnastics academy. When the business venture encountered economic problems, the Karolyis bought out their investors and have owned "Karolyi's Camp" ever since.

TRUDI LACEY

"To stick to it and never, ever give up. That was my mom's mantra. To persevere through everything and things will work out. And that's basically how I live my life."

Coach Lacey stuck with basketball. She was an assistant and head coach for twenty-two years, before being named head coach of the WNBA's Charlotte Sting in 2003.

MARVIN LEWIS

"To be yourself."

Coach Lewis is carving an identity as a confident, aggressive coach, and the Bengals, which have been long one of the NFL's worst teams, are on the rise.

LUTE OLSON

"Always try to be the best that you can be, and don't base that on what other people are.

"And the second thing that really stuck with me was when I was a young guy and had a job. There was this gentleman who had started a business from scratch and really made something out of it. He told me, 'Let me give you one piece of advice—the definition of a failure is someone who leaves for tomorrow what could be done today.'"

Olson expects the same work ethic from his players that he demands of himself. His late wife, Bobbi, once said, "He is the hardest worker I've ever seen and he expects the same from his players. He told me how he went out during practice recently and told one of the players, 'If you're going to practice like this, you might as well leave right now. You're a leader and you're going to affect everyone else on the court.'"

TOM OSBORNE

"In a coaching sense it was something I read in John Wooden's book, where he said that he never talked about winning. He always talked about the process.

"If you practice well every day and give a great effort, it's the daily, minute-by-minute acts that lead to performing well. And really after reading that, the last several years that I coached, I don't ever recall mentioning winning to our players either.

"Probably the most important advice that I got from my dad was to finish what you start. He had a good work ethic and he always wanted me to follow through on whatever I had begun."

John Wooden has written several books on coaching, leadership, and success, such as:

Wooden: A Lifetime of Observations On and Off the Court

Wooden on Leadership

Coach Wooden's Pyramid of Success: Building Blocks for a
   Better Life

BILL PARCELLS

"Probably the best advice I was ever given was from my dad. He said, 'One of the more difficult things to do is decide what you want. But decide what you want to do and then be willing to persist until you give yourself the best chance to achieve that.' In other words, he was talking about something I use with my teams all the time—staying power—to not have instant gratification; that's not what you should be expecting."

Parcells certainly has staying power. He's coached in the NFL for four decades, and has taken four different teams to the playoffs (the New York Giants, New York Jets, New England Patriots, and Dallas Cowboys).

MIKE SCIOSCIA

"The best advice I was given is that if you want to succeed and you want to achieve, you have to learn how to handle the failures. I think that's important in a lot of things, but especially baseball when there are so many things that don't go the way you want to leading up to an incredible moment. So I think being able to handle the failure is the only way you can learn how to achieve."

TUBBY SMITH

"The best advice I was ever given was probably from my dad. His whole thing was to do your job and your job only, and finish it. That was his whole thing, this military thing, growing up with seventeen brothers and sisters, everybody had chores and responsibilities, their own jobs to do. Just do your job. Do your job and finish it and everything else will take care of itself."

Smith's father was a farmer who raised his family in a cinder-block house with no indoor plumbing. The children had their own chores, such as picking fruit, stripping tobacco, hanging meat, feeding the animals, and milking the cows. Smith often spoke about instilling players with values—to teach them patience and perseverance, like he learned from his dad.

EMANUEL STEWARD

"I really wasn't given any shrewd advice; I'd say I pretty much was a guy who stumbled into success and made myself. I had no real mentors or anything. But the basic philosophy I've lived by is—usually, but not all the time—you get out of something what you put into it. That's what it comes down to. The best thing that you can do for anything in life is to be prepared. Preparation makes a big difference between success and failure. Stay focused and be prepared.

"Same as a lawyer. When a lawyer goes into a courtroom, he needs to be prepared. He may be the greatest lawyer in the world, but in this particular case he's out at the bars drinking, socializing with his friends while another little guy is at home studying his books, learning all the rules. And he comes into the courtroom prepared and comes out a winner over the great lawyer. Be prepared for everything. And last-minute preparation makes a big difference because it'll be fresh on your mind."

Steward then switched gears, talking about the innate intelligence he has seen in top athletes . . .

CK: "So effort overcomes talent sometimes."

ES: "Most of the guys that I've dealt with, the stars, are all very talented. It's amazing. All these guys—De La Hoya, Chavez, Lennox, Holyfield—they all are very talented. And they have an awareness of everything that's going on around them, which is interesting.

"They are all very intelligent, too. It's not just about college or education from books. I've seen guys become world champions who didn't possess this certain intelligence level and I would tell people, this guy's champion but I don't think he'll hold on to the title much longer."

JOE TORRE

"I can't think of any one startling thing somebody told me, but the revelation for me in what I do is, as you go along you learn and you correct and improve. To me, the whole thing is all about people. I was somewhat irresponsible in my young days and I think I corrected a lot of the things I didn't like.

"Then as far as dealing in the job I'm in, I try to apply psychology because there are a lot of times I get a reaction from players and I don't react to it. I sort of digest it and try to figure out what made them say what they said. I think the fact that I've been around this stuff so long, and watching other managers manage me, I was probably more aware of that than maybe a lot of people would be in their playing days."

We continued to talk about his maturing process . . .

CK: "That's an interesting development, an evolution."

JT: "Yeah . . . I think you learn as you experience. And to this or any job, you have to be believable, and to be believable it has to be something that is really deep-seated within you to be able to carry it off over a long period of time."

JOHN TORTORELLA

"I guess the best advice—and I'm not sure if it was given to me or what—but I have a piece of crystal on my desk and it's something I live by. It says, 'Dare to do what you dare to dream.' That's something I try to instill in our team and the way I live: Go for it. And no matter what people think and how you're doing it or what you're trying to do, if you feel it's something you want to go for, go for it."

The 2004 Lightning team won the Stanley Cup with a wide-open, free-wheeling style that was in stark contrast to the trapping, defensive hockey that has become commonplace in the play-offs. This exciting style reflected Coach Tortorella's "Go for It" philosophy. His team didn't clam up and play it safe, they rode speed and an explosive offense all the way to the Stanley Cup.

DICK VERMEIL

"Probably the day I got married at nineteen years old, my dad told me that no Vermeil had ever been divorced. So this commitment is for life. [Laughs.] And he was very serious. It's been forty-eight years and in terms of true value in my life, when someone asks me a question like that, that's what comes to my mind."

Coach Vermeil's wife, Carol, has always been an integral part of his players' development. He and Carol have welcomed players to their house for dinner on a weekly basis since Vermeil was coaching in high school. The Vermeils believe this ritual develops a familial bond that cannot be formed on the playing field alone.

BILL WALSH

"To find something you were extremely interested in and become the very best you could be in that area. In my case it was offensive football, so I just thrived on learning more and more about offensive football—concepts and theories and the practical application. So it's to really commit yourself to something you have a passion for. That's the best advice I ever received."

LENNY WILKENS

"That's hard to say, but one of the things that stuck with me from when I was a kid, my mother would always say, 'Let honesty and integrity define your character.' Another one was, 'Be accountable for what you say and what you do, because it's you doing it.'"

Although Coach Wilkens grew up in the rough Bedford-Stuyvesant section of New York City, his deeply religious mother educated him to stay away from the negativity surrounding him. Lenny focused on his schoolwork, eventually earning an athletic scholarship to Providence College and a ticket out of New York's mean streets.

JOHN WOODEN

"Listen to others."

When John Wooden was at Purdue University in the early 1930s, he listened to Coach Piggy Lambert. Wooden says, "He had the greatest influence on me both from the standpoint of playing and coaching. Coach Lambert had a fetish for details."

CHAPTER FOUR

OVERCOMING ADVERSITY

Y ou're not good enough. We don't want you. You can't play because you're a girl. You're too fat. You're not allowed because you're black. You're poor. You're damaged goods. These are all obstacles that people face every day. They're also hurdles each of these coaches faced and overcame in their lives. Not only did they overcome them, but many times these perceived setbacks provided the fuel that propelled them to great careers.

Many of the coaches' personal experiences touched and surprised me. The courage and love that Dan Gable showed when he moved into his sister's bedroom after she had been raped and murdered in the same room. Ken Hitchcock acknowledging his weight problem and eliminating it through hard work and exercise. Scotty Bowman sustaining a serious head injury at eighteen years of age that ended his playing days, but launched his second career as hockey's greatest coach.

Then eerily, when I was speaking to Trudi Lacey, she said something that echoed what my own father had told me years before, almost verbatim. She said people have times in their lives that are "defining moments," and they either propel you to greatness or they defeat you.

I had a bad year in 1995: I was young and cocky enough to think I could handle anything that came my way when life tested me. I had been living in Los Angeles for eight years when a series of sudden events shook me up emotionally. First, my father, who had been living in Los Angeles for five years, and was always there for guidance and advice, moved back East because my grandfather had become seriously ill. Second, my girlfriend, whom I'd lived with for five years, moved back to her hometown, San Francisco. We had broken up several months earlier, but when she moved away it officially ended the relationship. And then worst of all, one of my best friends sadly took his own life. He was troubled, and it was a complete and devastating shock.

I was in my midtwenties, and within a period of six months, I'd been separated from my father, broken up with my girlfriend, and lost a dear friend. At this point, I began to question my belief in God, my career, and just about everything. I no longer had a foundation underneath me—nothing was certain anymore.

I came back to Philly on a much-needed vacation and during a talk with my father, he said almost the same thing Coach Lacey would tell me nine years later. He said that in his experience, whenever something really bad happened to a person, how they handled those tragedies or setbacks would have a huge impact on the rest of their lives. Some people spun out of control and couldn't handle it. Others weathered the storm and became stronger than they were before. Then my dad said something I'll never forget: "Follow your head and your heart and you'll be OK, because you're a good person." Those words helped bring me out of that dark period.

I believe what these coaches say, that through adversity you really find out who you are, but it certainly helps if you have someone strong and kind—like my father or Coach Lacey—to help you hang tough when life throws you some curveballs.

Can you give an example of how you overcame adversity to continue to pursue your dreams?

RED AUERBACH

"When I was playing ball at George Washington University I came from a junior college and I had a lot of problems making the starting lineup, and when I did, I was lousy in the first or second game, so I was benched. Next thing you know in a squad of eleven guys, I was the eleventh man. Next game or so I didn't get in, and I didn't say a word. I didn't say a word because I deserved it. I just worked harder than ever in practice. Then all of a sudden, we were going to play Army. Coach says, 'They got a guy named Broika. I want you to do a job on him.' He started me in that game and I started ever since."

Red Auerbach played for George Washington University from 1937 to 1940. His hard work on defense stuck with him, and he drafted perhaps the greatest defensive player in NBA history, Bill Russell, who was the centerpiece of eleven Celtics championship teams.

DUSTY BAKER

"I was a skinny kid growing up and I wanted to be a pro athlete. And people would tell me I'm too skinny or, you know, always tell me there was something I couldn't do. Something I couldn't achieve."

CK: "The odds are against you."

DB: "Well in their mind, not in mine. One time we had to do a report on what you wanted to do and the class laughed at me. My eighth-grade teacher told them not to laugh and told me that if I was dedicated enough and believed in myself to go ahead and pursue my dreams and not let anybody tell you what you can't do.

"You're constantly bombarded by negatives. More people tell you what you can't do rather than tell you what you can do.

"And I'll tell you another one of the best pieces of advice I had when I was at a crossroads between going to college and playing basketball or football, or signing a pro baseball contract. My parents had just gotten divorced. Hank Aaron told me when I got drafted by the Braves that if I had enough confidence in myself to be in the big leagues by the time my class would have graduated, to go ahead on [with baseball] and if not, to go to college. You don't think about the chance that you took sometimes until much later."

Home run king Hank Aaron was an established star with the Atlanta Braves when Baker joined the organization in 1968. After a promise to Baker's mother, Aaron took Dusty under his wing and gave the youngster guidance when he first entered the big leagues. Today, Baker often credits Aaron as his mentor.

Dusty Baker was the on-deck hitter when Hank Aaron hit his 715th home run to break Babe Ruth's all-time record.

BRIAN BILLICK

"I'm very lucky in that I haven't had to face a great deal of tragedy. What I have been through—as a lot of people in my profession have—is I've been cut as a player twice, with the 49ers and the Dallas Cowboys. And that is a traumatic time for any young man to realize that the things you aspire to just aren't going to happen that way.

"I've been fired as a coach, just like every coach. You're not a coach unless you've been fired at one time or another. As a young coach, I had a job at San Diego State and after five years I got let go there. I had a new baby at the time. I hate to classify that as a trial and tribulation because it's so commonplace. It's nothing compared to the personal tragedies some people overcome. I've been lucky that way. But clearly, from a professional standpoint, overcoming rejection—the fact that at some point somebody told you that you're not good enough to do this—is always a lot to overcome.

"I try to keep that in mind and be very cognizant of it when I have to cut players, because I know what a devastation it was for me as a player. And I hope I don't become so callous in this business that I lose that memory or feeling of what it was like for me to go through that."

Being fired is an everyday reality for NFL coaches. In 1980, the average tenure for a coach with one team was almost five years. Today the average is less than three years.

NICK BOLLETTIERI

"Adversity really shows the true character of people. It's quite easy to do things when everything goes right. But when things happen that you don't expect to happen and you get yourself in the frying pan, and you never expected it because everything was going right, that to me really brings out when you are truly something special. Adversity, change of directions, impromptu decisions—that to me really determines what type of person you are. When you are involved in adversity and can come out ahead."

CK: "Was there a specific instance, anything in your life that you can think of?"

NB: "No, I think it's been my whole life, not just anything specific. When you try new things like I've done. The academy, summer camps, putting people on the road, building something that nobody else has in the whole world. It's the trying of new things. That's been my whole life, not just one thing. You accomplish something, then go out and do something else.

We've gone from tennis to golf to basketball to football. It's the new things. I keep trying new things all the time."

At its peak in 1987, the Bollettieri Academy boasted thirty-two students in the main draw at Wimbledon and twenty-seven in the U.S. Open.

BOBBY BOWDEN

"That's a darned good question because I think adversity is involved in everything. The biggest thing is that I came through coaching. I'll never forget the first head coaching job I got; I was twenty-five years old and I was the head coach at South Georgia College. We won our first game, then we won our second game. And all of a sudden I'm thinking I might not *ever* lose a game. [Laughs.] Man, I am the answer to the coaching profession. [Laughs.] We played the next game and got beat 61 to about 20 and now I'm beginning to wonder if I oughta even be in the profession. [Laughs.]

"And I've been on the verge of quitting, but what else would I rather do? I'd rather do this than anything in the world. So we stay with it, but there's been three or four times in my career where I was faced with that question and each time I'd say, 'I'd rather do this than anything else.' That's how I got through adversity."

Bowden never quit, and has coached the Florida State Seminoles since 1976, winning two national championships.

SCOTTY BOWMAN

"Well, I played amateur hockey up in my hometown, and where I came from it was a hockey hotbed, so even though there were only six teams at the time, I thought I was destined to play in the NHL.

"But I got injured. I suffered a career-ending injury when I was about eighteen, and my hopes were crushed to be a player. But I was fortunate and actually I was offered to continue my schooling by the team. Montreal offered to look after my schooling and then I was able to start in the coaching ranks at a much younger age.

"Normally people finish playing and then take up coaching, but I finished playing so young that I took up coaching and I was over ten years younger than most of the other coaches. So I got a head start, so to speak. And I was always used to coaching players around my same age.

"So it was an adversity when I first found out I wasn't going to play anymore, but it turned out to be the opposite of adversity. I got into coaching at a young age and that's always a break when you do something at a young age."

In a 1951 play-off game while with the Junior Canadiens, Scotty Bowman's skull was fractured when defenseman Jean-Guy Talbot hit him over the head with his stick. The injury ended Bowman's playing career and expedited his arrival on the coaching scene. Ironically, years later Bowman would coach Talbot with the St. Louis Blues.

JOHN CHANEY

"First try to understand that there are more don'ts in our lives than dos. I mean, Mama always said, 'Don't do this, don't do that.' Every time I wanted to go out, stay out late—you can't, don't. And every time you want to do this or that—you can't, don't.

"And all of it stems in so many ways not only from what they believed in how you should be raised, but also as a result of a lack of money. You didn't have money. Economics was a problem. If you think about that, in your life there are stop signs everywhere you go, coming from your parents as well as the neighborhood. Things we couldn't do in our neighborhood. There were always don'ts.

"I would have to believe that when I looked at it, from the standpoint of living in poverty, I just knew that this was something I didn't want. Many of us, most of us, move in a direction toward whatever, whether it's a good direction or bad direction, depending on what we want out of life or what we don't want. I didn't want to live in an area filled with poverty. I didn't want to live in a rat-infested area with roach-infested houses. I wanted to get out of that. I didn't want to live in a neighborhood where we were extremely poor.

"I knew I didn't want to be in the gangs, I knew I didn't want to be involved with guys who were bad guys, living in a house where there were roaches and rats, living in a neighborhood where there was crime and there were so many problems of poverty and so much of what you don't have. I wanted to just get away from that, so I went in an opposite direction, almost like an ant in terms of trial and error behavior, if you know what I mean.

"That's the way life is for some people, and especially for me. That's the way it was for me. The only thing I wanted to do was play basketball forever. I just wanted to dribble and shoot forever."

Chaney used basketball to escape Philly's mean streets. As a coach, he used it as a tool to help other less fortunate kids find their way to a better life through his work in the community, his Temple basketball program, and coaching clinics.

BILL COWHER

"Number one, coming out of college I was cut by the Philadelphia Eagles in 1979. I went back down and got in school and I was able to make the Cleveland Browns the following year as a rookie. I've always been kinda the guy who's been the bubble player. Then I had three surgeries and played five years, so I don't think I was ever a real gifted athlete and I always tried to get by on being dependable, being consistent, and trying to do something extra that could give me an edge."

In 1979, Cowher signed as a free agent with the Philadelphia Eagles, but was the last linebacker cut before the season started.

He played for the Cleveland Browns from 1980 to 1982, then went back to the Eagles from 1983 to 1984, where he was named MVP of their special teams unit in 1983. In 1984 a knee injury ended his playing career.

ANNE DONOVAN

"Professionally I think the biggest challenge of my coaching career was when I was in Charlotte. I was brought in as the new head coach to turn that franchise around, and we started the season 1–10. I came in preaching that we're a defensive team, we're gonna shut people down—and teams were scoring in the eighties on us every night.

"The lesson to me was there is a lot of pressure in the professional world where you don't get too long to prove yourself. I was able to keep the players in my camp committed to what my vision was for that franchise . . . and we turned that season around, and ended up in the WNBA Finals. It was just a proud moment for me that we were able to overcome really great odds to not only get to the play-offs, but then one by one knock off teams and get into the finals. It was very much unexpected from our group."

In 2001, Coach Donovan turned the Charlotte Sting around, going from a 1–10 record to start the season to an appearance in the WNBA Finals, where they lost to the Los Angeles Sparks.

ANGELO DUNDEE

"I was the last of the boys and I used to get the hand-me-downs from my brother Jimmy. I used to have to walk to school and all that my whole life, forget about driving. But nothing unusual. That's life, you take it in stride and learn from it. There's nothing wrong with that kind of stuff. We all have our faults and you try to overcome them by doing the right thing in life."

Dundee's straight-arrow ways set him apart as one of boxing's most honorable men. He always did the right thing for his fighters.

TONY DUNGY

"My second year in Pittsburgh with the Steelers I got sick. I got mononucleosis at the onset of training camp, and I missed about four or five weeks. Just sitting there recovering with nothing but rest and the medicine, it became very frustrating because I wasn't able to practice, wasn't able to do the things that I had always done. But it made me examine my priorities. Made me realize that football was important, but it wasn't the most important thing. And I think just reflecting on everything, that God had given me the benefits that I had, and the blessings that I did have, made me realize that it could all be taken away very quickly and very easily. It was something that I couldn't control and I think that when you realize that you can't control everything, it gives you inner peace, number one, but it also makes you focus on the things you can control. That was something that was really good for me in 1978.

"I got a peace of mind that put me more in touch with my religion and Christianity and depending on God. Then when I did come back it gave me a sense that there are some things that I can control. Let me do the best that I can with those and leave the other things to the Lord."

Tony Dungy is the antithesis of many modern-day coaches. He is humble, quiet, and poised, with an almost imperturbable presence. He rarely raises his voice and never curses.

HERMAN EDWARDS

"People will sometimes try to define your expectations and say what you can do and what you can't do. I was smart enough to figure out that you set your own expectations in life.

"And you're gonna have roads that are not always smooth. My dad used to always say, 'You don't quit when you're tired, you quit when the job is done.' There are going to be times when you don't feel real well and things aren't going your way, but you have to understand that the job's not done. Your job is your goal. You've got to get the job done. You've got to keep going and persevere.

"And for me, it was knowing that I was going to try to accomplish something coming out of where I grew up that a lot of guys had never done. First of all, to get a scholarship to go to a major college, then to go on to play professional football—that was my aspiration when I was eight years old. I was going to be a pro football player. No one was going to stop me from doing that. That was my ambition; that's what I wanted to do. Now did I know at eight years old how hard it was going to be? No, but I had that vision of doing that. I was going to be on TV and be a pro football player."

Coach Edwards continued on about his focus on reaching the NFL . . .

CK: "No matter what."

HE: "[Laughs.] No matter what. And I wasn't going to let anybody talk me out of it. And it wasn't always a straight road. I went to two colleges, didn't get drafted, was a free agent and all of that stuff, and that didn't hinder my ambition and passion for what I wanted to do. I stuck with it, and at the end of the day, I figured out that there are a lot of people that help you when you go through that adversity."

JEFF FISHER

"The first difficult situation that I faced was in college when I was literally injured for the first two and a half years of my college career at Southern California [USC] and was pretty much written off as one of those people that came in as a football player and then was eventually going to become a trainer.

"And I spent a great deal of time and really never gave up. I just kept working through it and working through it and developed myself physically to the point where I could compete. And I never had been given the opportunity to do so after what had happened.

"Secondly, I have a birth defect that's not widely known. I have a 95 percent loss of hearing in one ear. So I've basically gone through my career only being able to hear in one ear—which obviously has its benefits sometimes. [Laughs.] Being on the sidelines when I have the headphones on, I can't hear anything. Or when I need to sleep, I can sleep anyplace.

"You just have to work through those things—working through adversity is all about adjusting."

Coach Fisher worked through his adversity. He overcame injuries to play on USC's 1978 national championship team in the defensive backfield, alongside future NFL All-Pro players Ronnie Lott, Joey Browner, and Dennis Smith.

DAN GABLE

"On a daily basis you'll have small markers, but you usually can use them. That's one of the keys to my success—I pick up on a lot of things that would go over some people's heads, or go in one ear and out the other. They could be small or big and I'm going to go to a few real quick that are hard or big.

"In my life there were three major markers of adversity:

"I had a lot of success, so the day-to-day success helped me. But every once in a while there was a major setback. And those setbacks can either make you or break you. Mine was after winning all through high school and college, I lost my last collegiate match after 181 matches. And it was going to overtake me. It took a powerful group around me to bring me back and get me on the right track. I overcame this setback with the help of a great support group and I also had enough good things going day to day.

"Then, in coaching, after the Hawkeyes had won nine straight NCAA championships, we were going for the all-time record of ten, and we lost it. And there were a lot of changes I needed to make, that I had failed to make before that time, which caused that loss. But I didn't have the courage to do it before. And a real valuable lesson is that even when you're on top, you still need to make the needed adjustments to continue to stay on top.

"And then there are things that happen in everyday life. There's birth, there's life, and there's death. And in my family, we had a tragedy where my sister was raped and murdered in our own house. And that was going to overtake the Gable household. It was going to overtake Mom and Dad. I was fifteen at the time and I basically had to make some decisions and step up on behalf of the Gable family and help Mom and Dad and the family continue. And because I stepped up, they stepped up and started the healing process."

CK: "Did you start talking about it or something like that?"

DG: "Actually what happened was we stayed in the same house after quite a bit of discussion, but her room was, like, haunted. And I could see that after a month or so not much was getting accomplished from my parents' point of view. So I decided to move into her room and lived there for the rest of my high school career. Right where the murder had taken place."

In 1970, in his last match as a collegiate wrestler, Gable lost to Larry Owings, a sophomore from the University of Washington. Gable was ahead in the match by two points with twenty-five seconds remaining when Owings rallied for four points to win in the final moments. Gable avenged the loss when he later defeated Owings, and qualified for the Olympics.

BRAD GILBERT

"At sixteen, I was struggling. I dislocated my shoulder and was out about nine months. I was kind of feeling sorry for myself, you know. And I just learned at that point when things were down and I was moaning and bitching that I wasn't getting better, that I think that getting hurt actually helped me because it made me miss it. It made me put things in perspective. And when my shoulder got better, I had a little better attitude because I missed it. I took it for granted and I didn't realize I missed it until it was actually not there."

Coach Gilbert's attitude as a coach has matured from his early days. He now accentuates the positive and builds upon players' strengths, tailoring their games to capitalize on individual opponents' specific weaknesses.

CARRIE GRAF

"That's a good question because I think your ability to handle adversity is what makes successful people successful: taking things in stride, accepting criticism, and being able to critically self-evaluate. Those are the key ingredients in being able to handle adversity and to move forward. To say, 'This has happened, what can I do better? How I handle this will impact what I do next.'"

When pressed for specifics, Coach Graf touched upon the limitations put upon her because she was a girl . . .

CK: "Did anything happen to you personally as a woman athlete and coach—anything pop into mind?"

CG: "I think for me it was probably a lot of different situations growing up as a young female athlete where girls weren't meant to play sports, they weren't meant to play football; they weren't meant to get sweaty."

"That was something that impacted my life—when I was told I couldn't do something because I was a girl. And I wanted to go about changing that perception. It wasn't about gender, it was just about if I was good enough to do something, then I was going to go about trying to prove that."

APRIL HEINRICHS

"Adversity is different for different people. I don't believe in being a victim. Certainly in today's world there are victims of tragedies, death, disappointment, ACL tears. There are crimes that are committed on really wonderful and innocent people. But in general, I don't believe in staying in a victim's shell very often. So I have a hard time defining what adversity is.

"Most of my friends would say that my childhood was unlike theirs. And coming out of that childhood with the positive spin, the work ethic, the commitment to excellence and the drive and ambition that I had, is probably overcoming adversity."

Coach Heinrichs's work ethic as a player is well known in soccer circles. She was one of the most determined and hardworking players in U.S. women's soccer history and is credited with instilling the winning tradition on the U.S. national team that it is known for today.

WHITEY HERZOG

"I never had any adversity. I grew up as a poor man; I worked and supported myself from the time I was in seventh grade. I was very confident in what I was doing. I carried papers to make money; I carried lunches to make money. I didn't have a lot of talent. I signed with the New York Yankees, and was fortunate enough to make the big leagues. I don't call that adversity. I never dreamt I'd be a big-league baseball player, I certainly never dreamt I'd be a big-league manager."

Herzog got the most out of his own talent as a player and the most out of his players as a manager. The St. Louis Cardinals won three pennants and one World Series with teams that did not have the most gifted individuals, but they had the right combination of smart baseball players—a direct reflection of their wily manager.

KEN HITCHCOCK

"Well, I don't know if it's adversity, but I had two disadvantages as I was pursuing the things I wanted to do. And I didn't pursue things very hard, to be honest with you. I always have been happy wherever I've been. I don't really look to move on and I'm not really one of those guys who's looking for the pot of gold at the end of the rainbow.

"But the disadvantages I had were that I never played professional hockey, and that I was overweight. And I had to sell people every day that I had a feel for the game, I could coach, I wasn't afraid of the players, and the weight wasn't an issue.

"I couldn't control that I'd never played professionally, but I had to also show people that I was willing to train, work out, diet, and exercise to make myself a better human being. And be able to deal with the stress of our business better. So I did that. But I didn't do it to become an NHL coach—I was happy at junior, I was happy in the International Hockey League—I just did it because I wanted to be a better person. But I felt for a long time that I had to prove to people that because I never played that I could coach people that did play."

In the late 1980s, when he coached junior hockey in British Columbia, Coach Hitchcock weighed 450 pounds. His doctor told him if he didn't lose weight, he'd be dead in six months. By the time he was offered his first NHL head coaching job with the Dallas Stars, Hitch weighed a svelte 220 pounds.

BELA KAROLYI

"Adversity and obstacles are very common in everyone's life. And in my life, yes, I've had several of them; two major ones back in the old country [Romania] and one here in the new country [USA]. When I came to this country I found myself like a newborn child, not knowing the language, not knowing the people, not knowing customs. And not knowing how to pump gas at the gas station. [Laughs.]

"These obstacles sometimes are so powerful and they look so major that many people give up under the pressure. And that's when you see human tragedy. It breaks your heart to see valuable people giving up and being weighed down.

"My major obstacle was when my wife and I decided not to return to Romania and stay in the United States after the pressure and conflict I had with the Romanian government. Giving up your profession, actually giving up your identity through your profession, was the hardest thing I've ever experienced. Working on the docks along with people I had never known. People that were not what I would call on my standards. People that I wondered if part of them were human beings. Looking so strange, some unbelievable creatures I found there. I believe that was the most powerful and at the same time frightening event of my life.

"With all of that, one thing I never lost in front of me was that one day I'm gonna get through. I've got to fight through this situation and one day I'm going to get back into the profession I love so much. That was the idea that I followed to fight through. I have to make it through. I will not stay here. I will not get swallowed by the swamp. And actually that is how I got out of there."

CK: "Wow, so when you first came to the United States from Romania, you had to work on the docks?"

BK: "Yes."

CK: "Not very nice people down there?"

BK: "Well, I called it at the time the trashpile of humanity. Because definitely they look like it and they act like it. The big majority are not meant to be trash, but they became trash by giving up. By giving up hope. And that's when the swamp swallows you.

"I met people with great reputations, even from my old country. An electronic engineer with a big name in Romania.

I found him in a deplorable situation. Drinking the few pennies that he made along with me on the docks, giving up completely the hope that he would ever get out of there. I've seen musicians, great musicians from Poland that I've seen over there. That was probably the most powerful incentive, besides my own desire to work through this situation and get out. Seeing these valuable people in that condition."

CK: "So they inspired you to get out of that situation."

BK: "They were very frightening examples. Yes, it was great incentive."

Karolyi struggled after defecting to the United States. While working on a painting crew, he bumped into gymnast Bart Conner at the Los Angeles airport. Conner put him in touch with his coach, Paul Ziert, who helped Karolyi get his first coaching job in the United States.

TRUDI LACEY

"You have times in your life that you would call defining moments. They define who you are. They either propel you to greatness or they defeat you.

"A challenge that I had was when I lost my mom. I was heartbroken and devastated. You know up until that point I had no idea what it meant to have your heart broken. And four years after that I lost my father. So, that was an extremely difficult time.

"What I learned from that experience was that no matter what happens, you can find some good in it. In Romans 8:28 it talks about all things and working through it. So during that period when I was heartbroken, I searched for something good that had come out of losing my parents. What I came up with was that my parents had dedicated their entire lives so me and my sister could live a better life. And it made me recognize what I was supposed to do with my own life. That I was supposed to help as many people as I could live their best life. And that is how I define my purpose in living."

Romans 8:28
"And we know that for those who love God all things work together for good, for those who are called according to his purpose."

MARVIN LEWIS

"I had my scholarship taken away in my freshman year in college, so I had to fight to get it back to where I wasn't paying for my education. There was a coaching change when that occurred."

Coach Lewis attended Idaho State, where he earned All–Big Sky Conference honors as a linebacker for three years (1978–80). He received his bachelor's degree in physical education in 1981, and his master's degree in athletic administration in 1982.

LUTE OLSON

"Well, my father died when I was five, and I had an older brother, Amos, who was away at school, he was nineteen, I think, at the time. He came home to run the farm and was killed in a tractor accident eight months later.

"So, it was a case then of my mother and the three of us. My mother had an eighth-grade education, which was not unusual for women at that time. Everyone had to do their part for the family to survive. And it was not anything that you really thought about, it was just a fact of life. Everyone had to have a job and you did whatever kind of work you could in order to make ends meet.

"If I was going to get my college education, it was going to come through opportunities that athletics would bring me. And that's what ended up happening.

"But I never looked at it like it was something that I was going to have to overcome. It was more a case of I knew what I wanted to do, and it was just a matter of doing that in order to be able to teach and coach, which is what my goal was."

Coach Olson spoke of his mother's strength when I asked about the family tragedy . . .

CK: "You had some real family tragedy and I'm sure you look back at it now and see that you were pretty resilient."

LO: "The person that I've thought back on so much is my mother, because she was forty-seven years old and all of a sudden her oldest son was gone. I was five and my brother was nine or ten, and I had a sister that was about fourteen. So it's amazing how she was able to do everything that she did. She worked two jobs as well as running the household. It's just amazing."

TOM OSBORNE

"We had trouble with Oklahoma early in my coaching career. I think we lost the first five times we played with them. That was a big game in Nebraska, so it was kind of like Ohio State vs. Michigan, or USC vs. UCLA."

CK: "The Hatfields and McCoys."

TO: "Yes, and it was something that became a big thing to the fans. We had to just keep plugging, and finally in 1978 we beat them. And then I think from 1978 on we held our own or maybe a little bit more than held our own. But early on it was difficult. There was always a lot of pressure to change; to throw the ball more, to do something different and I always felt that when we had good enough players and when the ball bounced right we would win.

"We had a little bad luck with them early on, a couple of games we could've won that we didn't, so it taught me to pretty much stay the course and to have a philosophy. And as long as it made sense, to stick with it. That doesn't mean you never changed, but you didn't go with the wind either."

Nebraska's archrival is the Oklahoma Sooners. Early in Coach Osborne's career, he had little success against the Sooners, losing to them from 1973 through 1977. Nebraska fans called for Osborne's job on more than one occasion, until 1978, when Nebraska got the monkey off Osborne's back and defeated number-one ranked Oklahoma 17–14.

BILL PARCELLS

"The thing that happened to me happened pretty much all at once. I was named the head coach of the Giants in 1983, and that first year things went very, very poorly, including some tragic things in my personal life.

"Both of my parents died within a six-week period during that year. My mom died during the season; my father right after the season. A guy that I had driven to work with every day for almost six years, a coach that I had coached with in college named Rich Doughery, was killed in a plane crash. Then one of my assistant coaches with the Giants, a fellow named Bob Ledbetter, had a stroke and died.

"And this was all during a season that was going very poorly. Then after the season, I found out that the organization was looking around at another coach. And from one year—which, quite frankly, retrospectively now, after what they'd seen—I really don't blame them. However, I did blame them at the time.

"But I did get another chance, fortunately, to continue. And then

I kind of just altered the way I did things from that point on. I became much more focused, much more determined, much more aggressive, with much more of me trying to impose my will into the situation. And it worked for me. It worked. Things started going a lot better then. That was probably the low point for me."

In 1984, Parcells rebounded from the heartbreak he experienced the year before. He coached the Giants to a 9–7 record and a play-off berth. Two years later, in 1986, they won their first Super Bowl in a 39–20 thumping of the Denver Broncos. Giants quarterback Phil Simms was named MVP.

MIKE SCIOSCIA

"If you're pursuing a career in professional athletics, injuries are going to be a part of it, setbacks are going to be a part of it, and I've had my share of major injuries when I was young.

"When I was nineteen I had my knee operated on. I tore cartilage in it and although that wasn't career threatening, it definitely set me back at the time. Then, three years later, I tore my rotator cuff, which was career threatening. And it actually did end my career, but fortunately it was not until twelve years later."

Between injuries, Scioscia was an extraordinarily durable catcher. He caught one hundred or more games ten times in his career, and is the Dodgers all-time leader in games caught with 1,395. In spring training in 1993, he reinjured his shoulder, ending his playing career prematurely.

TUBBY SMITH

"I don't know about 'overcome,' I just think there are always challenges that you have. I guess being from where I'm from, from a rural poor area in southern Maryland—and I never thought of us as being poor—but I think being willing, being able, being fearless in my ability to just pursue things, just to move away.

"Because I've always had good health, had a good family. Mom and Dad have always been there. So I've been really blessed in that regard. I don't think I've had any real tragic episodes or racial encounters or anything like that to overcome. I mean you have monetary problems, but that's not anything unique. But there's not one thing I can pinpoint in getting over it and how I did it."

We went on to talk about his financial adversity . . .

CK: "Well, the economics is really a form of adversity."
TS: "But you don't really realize it. That's all you know [at the time]."
CK: "But now you can look back and see."
TS: "Oh, now I can look back and see what it was."

EMANUEL STEWARD

"I have an attitude that there is a solution for every problem God puts on you. He doesn't put anything on your shoulders bigger than you can handle. And I've had major problems, even just in general. Just being from a fatherless home. My parents divorced, lived in Detroit. They had to struggle or whatever, but I never dwelled on negative things or my problems. I just kept working. And working and working and working.

"Even right now when I have things that go bad I believe that everything is a temporary situation. I deal with it that way. You live your life and you're going to have rainy days and you're going to have sunny days. Everything is going to change. Life is steadily evolving, alternating currents like electricity. And when anything in life is extremely, extremely good, be prepared, because it's going to have to turn. That's part of life. It'll come back and turn and not be so good. And if it's extremely, extremely bad, just hold on. Stay humble and keep working because you could be on a winning streak and doing everything that's right and all of a sudden you run across a spot where every damn thing seems to go wrong. It happens. Just be prepared to survive it. You ever go to my Web site?

CK: "Yes, I've seen the Kronk Gym Web site [www.kronkgym.com]."

ES: "We have the story of when I came to Detroit and all that. We had it pretty rough but I just kept working all the time, I never dwelled on my problems. Keep on working, keep on working."

When he was eleven years old, Steward's parents divorced. His mother, Catherine, packed up the family's belongings and moved the family from West Virginia to Detroit, Michigan. The young Steward, with his Southern accent, didn't exactly fit in in his new hometown and began to fight for respect.

His mother tried to get him out of these street fights, and directed her son to enter the Catholic Youth Organization's gym and resume the boxing he had begun back in West Virginia. Emanuel followed his mother's orders and later became a Golden Gloves champion.

JOE TORRE

"I think I have to go to one person, and that's my wife, Ali. And first off the dream that seemed to be the most important to me, going back to my playing days and even before that when I was a teenager and my brother Frank played for the Milwaukee Braves, and played in two World Series, both in 1957 and 1958 against the Yankees. And the one thing that I felt was the most important or significant thing you could do as a baseball player was be in the World Series. I guess that's always been a motivator for me. Even though I won the MVP of the league in 1971 and led the league in hitting and stuff, it wasn't enough because it wasn't a team effort, it was an individual thing.

"My playing career ended in 1977 and I became the manager of the Mets and managed there for five years. Then I went to Atlanta and we went to the postseason in 1982, my first year there. We got knocked out by the Cardinals, who went on to win the World Series. I got fired by the Braves after three years, and I remember sitting at the kitchen table with my wife, and she said, 'How do you feel about yourself?' I said, 'I feel like someone who never realized their dream.' And then she proceeded to chew my rear end off. She wouldn't stand for the fact that I was giving up on the rest of my life.

"It was from that point on that I got into different things. I went on to be a broadcaster and she got me concentrating more on taking better care of myself and working out, which really translates into higher self-esteem. As you start feeling better, you start thinking better about yourself. And it's been an ongoing process for us, but I think that probably was the turning point for me in gaining another level."

After this low point in his managing career, Torre went on to manage the St. Louis Cardinals from 1990 to 1995. Then, in 1996, after sixteen seasons as a major-league manager, he finally realized his lifelong dream of winning the World Series in his first year as skipper of the New York Yankees.

JOHN TORTORELLA

"When I took over the Rochester Americans in the American Hockey League—and we ended up winning the championship that year—my first few months there I ended up retiring an icon in Jody Gage. I'm not sure if you're familiar with him or not, but he was a very big name in that city. And it was my first job after I was an assistant with the Buffalo Sabres for six years. I did it because I felt he couldn't play anymore and just couldn't make our hockey club at that time. No one else ever wanted to do that and I think it pretty much turned the city against me. [Chuckles.]

"It's a pretty tough city and as it turned out it was such a great experience the two years we spent there, but I was hung in effigy. And there was a tremendous amount of adversity there—for my family, when they went to the rink, when I went to the rink. But we ended up winning the Calder Cup that year and I think again, believing that you're doing it the right way and believing in the team first was my philosophy in that situation.

"And the same thing happened with a young man here in Tampa with Vinny LaCavalier. We've had a very tenuous relationship in trying to teach him the team concept and there was quite a bit of adversity there with people calling for my job. You know, everybody's calling for my job every year as every coach usually has happen to them.

"But again, that type of adversity, when people are coming at you and questioning you and want you out, whether it be public, media, or whatever, that can affect you. You've got to close within yourself and ask yourself, 'Is this the way it should be done for the best of the team?' And if you answer the question 'Yes' then you need to go with it. All decisions should be made for what's best for the hockey team, or for any sports team. And if you answer that question 'Yes' then you need to go with it, no matter what may happen. And you could lose your job over that. But you still can't bend and try to please everybody.

"I think those are two very similar things that happened as far as adversity in a coach-player relationship—Jody Gage and me in the American League and Vinny and I in the National Hockey League. But they transformed themselves and we found our way."

CK: "Just listening to you, that translates to a lot of different things. In my mind when you were talking I translated it to marriage. If you are arguing with your wife and you think something, you have to pretty much [stick to it]. You know what I mean?"

JT: "Well, marriage isn't an easy thing. You're going to have disagreements, but if you try to just throw it in the corner and have it hide somewhere, it's going to fester into a major problem later on."

CK: "Right."

JT: "That may just break everything as far as the family or whatever it may be. But I think, Christian, if you meet these problems head on as they come at you then it doesn't turn into a big, festering conflict."

CK: "Building up, building up . . ."

JT: "Yeah, yeah, especially in our business, as far as a coach when you're dealing with players and media and management and all that. If you hide from these problems, and maybe even lie your way through it and try to please everybody, it's going to come back and hit you square in the face.

"I think when you meet the conflict head on, as you go through that process of trying to get through that conflict, you and that party become closer and tighter. It may not be great at that particular time, but you work through it together and you become closer and tighter as you go through maybe months of the problem. I have a true belief in that and I've seen it work. That's a constant belief of mine."

CK: "I agree. Some people are afraid of confrontation or want to avoid it."

JT: "Absolutely, absolutely and it comes back and kicks you right in the balls. [Laughs.]"

Coach Tortorella has a straightforward style that reflects the mentality of the hearty city of Boston where he grew up. His work with Vinny LaCavalier paid off, and LaCavalier has developed into one of the best players in the NHL.

DICK VERMEIL

"Well, I had to leave the National Football League and coaching after seven years as head coach of the Philadelphia Eagles because I was burnt out and on a very close edge of having a real emotional breakdown. And it was because of the kind of personality I have, double or triple A, whatever it may be. Being consumed by the profession and the desire to excel.

"So I left; I had to leave. I left it for fourteen years. That's probably the most critical time of my life, and every year for the next fourteen years except for one, I was offered an opportunity to consider going back and actually was told, 'The job is yours' four different times, but I never interviewed until that fifteenth year.

"Well, I interviewed once—the Philadelphia situation in 1996."

CK:　"What was it that made you come back, that finally got you over the hurdle?"

DV:　"First, when I got involved in the true interview process with the Eagles and I recognized that it wasn't the best thing for me to do, I then also realized that I still had the passion to coach and I felt that I could control the passion to excel. I felt in control of myself enough to go back and do it."

CK:　"A little older, a little more mature?"

DV:　"A lot more mature."

When Coach Vermeil left the Eagles in 1982 he was burnt out, having been one of the most intense, emotional coaches in league history. His face was agonizing to watch on the sidelines when the Eagles were losing.

Many years later, he's still emotional, but he has mellowed considerably.

BILL WALSH

"Well, I think I was overambitious early in my career. It took some maturing. I would say it took me five or six years to totally mature as a coach and begin to focus on what I was doing rather than where I was going in coaching—whether I was going to be a head coach or what job I had. And at some point I came to the realization that the only way to thoroughly enjoy it is to focus on the level you're coaching and be the very best at that level. And everything else takes care of itself.

"So from that standpoint I became a serious coach and things began to work that much better for me."

Walsh expanded on the struggle to become an NFL head coach . . .

CK: "When you stopped thinking about where you were trying to get to."

BW: "Exactly, and that's typical of young people who don't know. They would like to be that character, that athlete, that entertainer, and in working toward getting there, they're not quite willing to make those sacrifices. In reality if you truly thrive on your work and have a passion for it and enjoy going to your job every day, then things can't help but work out for you.

"It took me a long time to ever break out of being an assistant football coach. And there were many, many years that I wondered if I'd ever become a head coach."

CK: "So you had doubts along the way."

BW: "I had the frustration that I may never get the opportunity."

LENNY WILKENS

"We have to overcome adversities all through life. I can remember early in elementary school, there were times when we didn't have nice clothes and didn't dress as nice as everyone else. And you could see people laugh or say things. But I always felt OK, because Father Mannion was always around to say clothes don't make the man or the person. So I wouldn't let it bother me.

"I can remember in high school we had some teachers who weren't very good, and they would tell the whole class that we should get out and get a manual labor job. Even in college I can remember dating a white girl, and her mom didn't have a problem with it, but her dad did. And he had a priest talk to me up at school. I went to Providence College and we had Dominican priests. I didn't know this guy really well, but when he started to talk to me, I questioned him. I said to him, 'You know you're a man of God. How can you come to me and talk to me about something like that? If anyone shouldn't see color, it should be you.' And he didn't know what to say. He started to say some things about society and I said, 'Well, you're the people who make society.'

"So you have experiences along the way. I can remember when I was a rookie with the Hawks, after my first year I had gotten married and we bought a home out in an area and 'For Sale' signs went up everywhere. Some people moved. Some people stayed, and we became friends and had a chance to have some dialogue. But I wasn't going to let someone else define who I was, just because of their ignorance."

Wilkens, whose father was African American and his mother Irish American, often encountered racism as an NBA player and coach. Through basketball he escaped the poverty of his youth and, as a Hall of Famer as both a player and coach, rose above the prejudice and racism he encountered.

JOHN WOODEN

"When I went to Purdue I wanted to be a civil engineer. But there were no athletic scholarships in my day and my parents didn't have the means to help me financially. So I knew I'd have to work my way completely through. I knew I had to work in the summertime. And after my freshman year, toward the end of the year I found out I'd have to go to civil camp every summer. I knew I couldn't do that because I had to work, so I just changed to a liberal arts course, majored in English, and I knew from that time I was going to teach. And I never looked back."

This decisive career change produced one of the greatest teachers of the twentieth century.

CHAPTER FIVE

QUALITIES FOR SUCCESS

Michael Jordan, Joe Montana, and Larry Bird all possessed a quality that set them apart from their competition. When you watched them, it was obvious they were the smartest player in the game. In their primes, they reached the equivalent of genius-level intelligence and awareness in their chosen fields.

How did they achieve this?

Jordan, for all his electrifying athletic ability, didn't win a championship until he figured out how to control the game's tempo and shut down opponents with an aggressive trapping defense in tandem with backcourt mate Scottie Pippen. He also developed a marksman's jump shot to compliment his dazzling driving ability. He eventually became a complete player.

Montana wasn't the prototypical quarterback by physical standards. He was not tall and his arm was weaker than his contemporaries John Elway and Dan Marino, but he was unflappable. He seemed to have antifreeze in his veins and was as accurate under pressure as William Tell. He also had the benefit of Coach Bill Walsh's fluid offense, and the game's greatest all-time receiver, Jerry Rice.

Larry Bird was slow and couldn't jump, but he could hit three pointers in the dark. In the clutch, he was the best shooter I've ever seen and could pass like a magician. At six-foot-nine, he used body positioning as well as anyone in hoops history. Bird also played with fellow Hall of Famers Robert Parish, Kevin McHale, and Bill Walton.

What we saw from these players was the result of years of effort and teaching—and persistent work. They were three of the most talented and hardest-working players ever. When that combination merges with the right teammates and teachers, the results are awesome.

All the coaches interviewed believe that work ethic, perseverance, and attitude were vital to becoming your best. But one coach, Emanuel Steward, went into detail about an innate intelligence common in all of the great athletes he'd encountered. He said it's not necessarily academic, just a natural intelligence that makes them aware of their surroundings. I agreed with him because of the guys I grew up with—the book-smart guys weren't always the brightest. In fact, some of them lacked common sense. Other intelligence indicators can't be measured by taking a test, and Steward believes this acumen is integral to whether or not a fighter will hold on to his crown.

Many athletes have equal physical gifts, but the ones who rise above the others have a better understanding of the game and their role in it. They figure out a way to make sure their *team* comes out on top. After listening to the coaches' answers, I think a successful person blends many qualities, and once you find what you love to do, and keep at it, you will rise to the level that your intelligence brings you to—and that in itself is success.

What is the most important quality a person needs to become successful?

RED AUERBACH

"It's when you feel satisfied with what you're doing and knowing that you're doing the best you can do. Doing your best and knowing it's your best."

Auerbach, who has been with the Celtics since 1950, let everyone know he was satisfied with his team's performance by lighting a "victory cigar" when he was certain they had sealed another victory.

This ritual became so reviled by other teams that the Cincinnati Royals management once handed out five thousand cigars to its fans, instructing them to light up when the Royals won. They never got the chance, however, as the Celtics easily beat them.

DUSTY BAKER

"Dedication, desire, and love for what you're doing. Because once you fall in love with what you're doing, then you explore other avenues and see things that you might not have seen before. I think you have to spend countless hours pursuing that, practicing, reading, doing whatever you can to learn more about what you're doing and more about yourself."

Baker's passion for baseball is well known throughout the major leagues. When Cubs president Andy MacPhail hired Dusty as manager, he cited Baker's popularity among players, stating, "He's an enormously popular manager with his players. As a result, the field of players that would like to play for the Cubs has increased with tonight's announcement by a large amount."

BRIAN BILLICK

"I guess if I had to narrow it down, to me it's conviction and passion. This goes back to your question about success—*you* have to define what that is. You've got to be completely honest with yourself. If you're true to yourself and you recognize that it is conviction and passion, that will usually overcome whatever inequities you might have intellectually, emotionally, mentally, and physically—in just about whatever you're trying to achieve."

Coach Billick feels a person needs to know where they stand on things . . .

CK: "You definitely have a confidence when you talk about it."

BB: "I've been through the baptism by fire when your conviction and passion for what you do is tested in the ultimate way. Because there are always going to be those that attack you and try to challenge that conviction. And it goes back to you knowing yourself. You better know who you are, what you have conviction about, and what you are passionate about."

NICK BOLLETTIERI

"Let me put it this way: You gotta have big cojones. You gotta have big balls, baby! If you don't have big balls and you're not willing to put it all out there on the line, against all odds, against everybody in life, then you can't make it. That's what it's all about. If you don't believe that you can accomplish what you're setting out to do, then you don't have a damn chance. It's the attitude. A-T-T-I-T-U-D-E. It's the attitude that you have that will determine success or failure most of the time."

Bollettieri's brash New York attitude makes him recognizable as one of the most opinionated and outspoken personalities in tennis.

BOBBY BOWDEN

"In my opinion, it's the ability to love and get along with others."

Bowden is a people person, and he loves meeting and being around others. His affection for people comes across to parents, making him a natural recruiter. Parents trust him to guide their children through four years of college.

SCOTTY BOWMAN

"Probably the most important thing is attitude. I really think that there are a lot of things you can't change, that are out of your control, but your attitude is in your control. The right attitude is something that will help you be successful. There are not many successful people that don't have the right attitude.

"There are other things you have to have: You have to have some patience, you have to have perseverance obviously, and you have to maybe have had some adversity too. But the main thing I'd say is attitude. You can always do something to help your attitude."

Bowman's reputation was as a no-nonsense disciplinarian, like a general at war. Because of this demanding style, former Canadiens winger Steve Shutt once admitted, "You hated him for 364 days a year, and on the 365th day you collected your Stanley Cup ring."

On a personal note, I found Coach Bowman to be friendly and engaging. He enjoyed our conversation and was pleasant to speak with.

JOHN CHANEY

"I think it's the kind of integrity that one should have, the honesty that one should have. And it cannot be tainted with a bad understanding of what the integrity of a sport is. You can't taint it. You can't allow somebody to accept success or to accept anything from anybody when you know it is in a dishonest form.

"What happens, though, is that too many of us as coaches measure people by the fact that the ball goes in the basket or you scored a touchdown or you won the race, as opposed to determining that this youngster was successful because he put forth the best effort, the best energy that he had and he was honest about it. There is a great deal of integrity in the way he goes about life and the way in which he participates in life.

"So I'm gonna say you've got to be honest, honest with yourself. And it's cheap, it's cheap to be honest. There's a higher form of integrity when you're trying to help and educate youngsters."

Coach Chaney believes so strongly in honesty and integrity that occasionally his temper spills over, putting him at odds with other coaches and collegiate officials.

BILL COWHER

"I think it's pride in their work. You'll never find a successful person who doesn't take pride in everything they do. It starts early. Once you are given your job, your chore, your mission at that time, successful people take pride and become the very best at what they are given at that time. That is what opens up the opportunities later on. The pride in your work."

Cowher took over one of the proudest franchises in the NFL and has carried on Pittsburgh's winning tradition for well over a decade.

ANNE DONOVAN

"The ability to overcome adversity. To enjoy the highs but be able to handle the lows and the challenges and to have the perseverance to get to the other side. To have the intelligence and the strength to get through the adversity."

As a child, Coach Donovan was teased and stared at because of her height. She didn't fit in. As an adult, she has turned this insecurity into a strength, becoming one of the world's best players and coaches.

ANGELO DUNDEE

"Be nice, it don't cost nothing. It's a cheap commodity and people react to that. There's no better thing than decency; getting to know your fellow man and enjoying them. And be realistic in what you're doing. That's all. Be nice."

One of boxing's most personable gentlemen, Angelo lived this motto.

TONY DUNGY

"You have to have self-motivation. You have to have vision—to be able to dream and set goals that everyone can't see. And then you have to have focus—to keep that in perspective and stay after your goals."

Coach Dungy has all of the above. He took over a foundering Tampa Bay franchise and turned the team around by developing the NFL's best defense. Now, with the Indianapolis Colts, he has motivated his personnel and is winning with an offensive machine.

HERMAN EDWARDS

"I would say perseverance. You have to have perseverance. You have to know that to gain success there are going to be tough times that test your character. And the things you do in the dark come to the light. All of those things come out of you when you're trying to achieve success. You find out who you are.

"And confidence is part of that. Confidence is the characteristic of a positive attitude regardless of the circumstances."

Coach Edwards persevered as a child from an interracial marriage who grew up in the civil rights era. His evangelical style of motivational speaking is becoming his trademark.

JEFF FISHER

"I believe there are two and both of them are related. Number one would be communication. You have to be able to communicate. Without it you have very little chance of being successful. And communication goes beyond just a one-way communication. For a head coach or assistant coach or an administrator, being able to express themselves is important, but to be understood is more important. Which leads me to the second aspect, which is listening. If you can't listen, you can't win, you can't be successful.

"And we have to differentiate and make sure that our athletes and our team, our staff understands the difference between hearing and listening. 'I got you coach, I got you coach,' where it goes in one ear and out the other, is hearing. Listening and retaining and understanding is critical. You cannot overemphasize listening enough. And the difference between the two."

Coach Fisher's communication skills make him a media favorite. In 2001, he won the Horrigan Award, given to the NFL figure who is most cooperative with the media. He is also cochairman of the NFL's Competition Committee, which implements rules changes and investigates ways to improve the game.

DAN GABLE

"This is hard because there are several, but one of them is the ability to read the situation at hand, to make the necessary adjustments, if they're needed, to flow through that time period. For example, when you're in a practice or in a match and something's there that can help, the ability to read it and make an adjustment right then— this is one of the most important qualities a person needs."

Wrestling technique is fundamental to winning, and Coach Gable is a master at making adjustments to counter or prevent opponents' moves, giving his wrestlers an incredible edge.

BRAD GILBERT

"An incredibly positive attitude. Incredibly humble. A hard worker. Dedication. Discipline. Desire."

CK: "You're the first coach to say humility. And from my own experience if you're not humble, nobody's going to want to be bothered with you."

BG: "Well, you could be a great coach and nobody likes you. See, I'm not that kind. Some guys are quick-fix guys. They come in, they scream, they get everything going for a little bit and then they'll burn out. I'm not like that so I can't identify with that, because I never liked that kind of attitude. I wouldn't want anybody to scream at me, or that whole thing. Screaming at somebody to challenge them."

CK: "Sounds like you have a different approach."

BG: "You know what I try to do? I try to maximize. It's not about me, it's about them. I do the best I can at helping them and I have a good idea that when they're out there [on the court], *they're* the ones out there. And I don't forget that. I'm not above the show. Sometimes coaches get above the show.

"You know who my coaching idol is? John Wooden. He is the greatest of all time in that he's humble. He has humility like nobody. When he talks about the 1964 team or the 1971 team, he will never say one team was better than another. He doesn't point out an individual, it's always about the team. Everything is about the team and about how you can become a better person. If you can work with a team you can work with others."

CK: "Coach Wooden said a great thing: 'Winning is a by-product of hard work. Success is a by-product of giving your best effort.'"

BG: "Success was like he saw it, in the practices. In the work ethic and everybody taking and doing their role."

A good example of this work ethic is the effect Coach Gilbert had on the transformation of Andre Agassi. Early in Agassi's career, his long hair and "Image Is Everything" ad campaign cast him as a player with more style than substance. Under Gilbert's tutelage, Agassi's work ethic and image made a 180-degree turnaround and he transformed himself into one of tennis's hardest working, most dedicated winners.

CARRIE GRAF

"Your ability to handle adversity. I think that makes or breaks people's success in life. That you can hit a barrier or hit a hurdle, and jump over it or go under it or go around it and continue to move forward. Your ability to handle adversity in a small situation or in a large one, in all areas of life and professional sports, hugely impacts your ability to succeed."

APRIL HEINRICHS

"That's a really tough one for me because I'm in a place in my life where clearly ten years ago I would have said work ethic. And that's certainly still in the top three, because without it I don't think anyone's very successful. It's probably the single greatest common denominator in all facets of life. Whether you're talking about a rap artist, or a soccer coach, or a businessperson, or a television anchor, I'm willing to bet that most successful ones would veer toward work ethic.

"But I've come to a place in my life now where I've seen charismatic people get far along in life without the work ethic. Strong leaders with charisma, but lack of follow-through skills or organizational skills or work ethic in terms of real commitment on a day-to-day basis—sometimes charisma can carry people a lot further in life. And you know, it goes back to that phrase: Sometimes it's not so much what you know—it's who you know. Charismatic people tend to be magnets for a lot of people.

"So it's a little bit of a conflict for me. I'm still going to go along with work ethic and a commitment to excellence along with the process of setting goals, reevaluating goals, and then pursuing goals. Those are the most important qualities."

Coach Heinrichs knows about work ethic and charisma. Her tenacious work ethic on the soccer field is legendary, and she played with and coached Mia Hamm, one of women's soccer's best and most charismatic players.

WHITEY HERZOG

"First of all, you gotta have a brain. In whatever you're going to become successful at in your profession, you have to have a thorough knowledge of what you're talking about, so when you try to get that across to people that are working for you or playing for you, they respect your knowledge. That's the first thing.

"The second thing is they have to know you're honest. You can't lie to them; they have to always know that whenever they hear you say something, it's the truth.

"Those two traits are most important because if they don't respect your knowledge in what you're trying to get across, or they might have any idea that you're not being honest with them, I don't think it's going to work."

Herzog's baseball smarts and honesty are what made him one of the game's best managers.

KEN HITCHCOCK

"You have to be believable. People that play for you and that you work for have to trust that you know what you're doing and that you have a plan to get there."

Coach Hitchcock thinks believability and passion can be more important than the coach's system. He has said that most systems will work if the players believe in the coach's passion and commitment.

BELA KAROLYI

"Perseverance. Definitely it's the most important because if you give up one time or back off one time, it will be extremely detrimental to success. Great perseverance: to continue to move toward your goal. This is the key ingredient to success."

An example of Coach Karolyi not backing off occurred in the 1996 Olympics. He instructed Kerri Strugg to complete her vault on a sprained ankle. The gymnast stuck her landing on one leg, sealing the gold medal for the U.S. team.

TRUDI LACEY

"Honesty—being honest with yourself about your strengths and also areas that you need to improve in. Looking at those honestly and working at them to get better. And secondly, being honest with the people around you in terms of communicating what you think and what you feel. Being honest, but not being brutal. When you communicate honestly and openly with people, it builds trust, it builds relationships. And the people that are most successful in life have the best relationships."

Coach Lacey's people skills elevated her to the positions of head coach and general manager of the Charlotte Sting, where she is responsible for all of the Sting's basketball operations.

TOM OSBORNE

"I would say sound character.

"I think long term, long haul. People who have integrity, whose word you can count on, who you know will work hard, who will be loyal—those are people who are more successful over a long period of time. You can certainly achieve some degree of economic success or material success in a short time by taking shortcuts. But usually, sooner or later, it catches up to you.

"I've talked a lot to our players about issues of character. We had a theme of the week that we talked about where one week it would be perseverance, another week it would be honesty, another week it would be self-sacrifice, another week it'd be courage, and we'd have a number of quotes by famous people about that topic. I'd talk to them about the theme and we'd have it in the scouting report. We'd talk about it on Monday and then talk about it again around Thursday and then again on Saturday morning on the day of the game. And how it related to having a good team and being a good player and what we were trying to get done. So in the course of going through thirteen games you really had talked about thirteen different themes and most all of those were character-related.

"It was really a course in character education that was never labeled as such. And hopefully, as coaches, we were able to model those traits most of the time. I think for the most part our team bought into it, and I think generally speaking we had a good level of character among our players."

This character-building experience came from Coach Osborne's personality. He led his teams with a quiet, humble confidence stemming from his strong religious beliefs.

BILL PARCELLS

"Integrity. You can't bullshit yourself, excuse the language. You need to have integrity. You know I read something about Warren Buffett one time where he said that having intelligence and ambition without integrity will kill you. [Laughs.] I think you have to be honest and forthright. I just think that's important."

Coach Parcells's frankness makes him one of the most quotable coaches in all of sports.

Warren Buffett is generally considered the world's most successful investor. He is the head of Berkshire Hathaway and is ranked by

Forbes *magazine as the second-richest person in the world, with an estimated net worth of $40 billion.*

MIKE SCIOSCIA

"I think it's perseverance. Keeping perspective to be able to have the patience you need, and also knowing when to really get up and get after something. But I think it comes down to perseverance.

"I don't know anybody that's just had a garden path where everything they touch turns to gold and they don't have any obstacles, any hurdles. I think, to achieve and become successful, the number-one attribute that is common to everyone I've talked to is perseverance. No matter what talent level they might have."

Scioscia persevered as a player. He missed most of the 1983 season due to a rotator-cuff tear that he suffered when throwing out San Diego Padres base stealer Alan Wiggins. However, he went on to play nine more seasons, including with the Dodgers 1988 world championship team.

TUBBY SMITH

"Honesty. If you have honesty people are going to trust you and believe in you. And I just think if you lie, you'll cheat; if you cheat, you'll steal; if you'll steal, you'll kill. . . . So it all boils down to honesty, which can be tough, because there are times when you have to really be careful.

"For example, as far as the media, you can't tell it all. You don't want to be dishonest, but there are certain things you can't talk about because there are other protocols. There are laws and rules that preclude you from being as forthcoming as you want to be. But if you're basically honest and sincere with people, they're going to know it. And *you're* going to know it. So you don't have to lay awake at night thinking, 'What did I say? What did I do? Did I do the right thing?' I couldn't exist like that."

Coach Smith's small-town values have made him successful at one of the nation's biggest basketball programs.

EMANUEL STEWARD

"First of all, you have to be disciplined, that's the first thing. If you don't have discipline, it's going to take away from your performance.

"The next thing a person needs to be is determined. Because everyone is going to have adversity and you need determination to keep on going. And then I think you have to be really focused.

"Mainly, it will have to be discipline. If you don't have discipline, you're not going to make it in anything.

"And one quality that I have found that is in all superstars is a certain innate intelligence. All champions have it. All of them. I don't care whether it's Michael Jordan, Roy Jones, or whoever, there's a certain intelligence they have in the ring and out. It's not necessarily academic. It may be a guy that's not educated, [it] may be a wild-streak-type guy or whatever, but there's something about them, the intelligence that they're born with.

"I've seen guys become world champions who didn't possess this certain intelligence level and I would tell people, this guy's champion, but I don't think he'll hold on to the title much longer."

Mr. Steward's intelligence seems to pass on to his fighters. The awareness he speaks of is evident in his insightful and intelligent analysis on HBO boxing broadcasts.

JOE TORRE

"Honesty. I know in the corporate world it's tough, but I think as opposed to misleading someone, you're better off not telling them anything. I try to be as open as I can with my players, and I don't always deliver good news. However, I always try to come at it from a positive side. If it's someone whose time I feel is gone as a player, I tell them how proud they should be of what they accomplished up to that point, and to take that with them where they're going now. Because all of a sudden they're young again; they're old as a player, but young as a person. You need to feel good about yourself. And to me it's fairness and honesty. And I'd like to believe that if my players are asked about that, then that comes out."

Torre's philosophical perspective comes from a lifetime in baseball. After a seventeen-year career as a player, he has enjoyed more than twenty-five seasons in his second career as a manager.

JOHN TORTORELLA

"To me, in business and in sport, it's mental toughness. I'll speak on my sport. It's not the Xs and Os, it's not the physical ability of the athlete—it's your mental ability, your mental mind-set. I think that is the most important thing in trying to get it figured out. It's mental. That's the toughest thing for people to understand, because everybody has a different mental mind-set."

Coach Tortorella took a Tampa Bay Lightning team known for its explosive offense and instilled in them the mental toughness necessary to survive the grueling NHL play-offs, en route to their first Stanley Cup title in 2004.

DICK VERMEIL

"Compassion for other people. I think a lot of the athletes we coach today come from almost dysfunctional families. And I think that the more they trust you and the more they respect you as a leader, then the more they're willing to work to be what they have the ability to be. I don't know if compassion's the right word, but I know it's a high priority.

"And I automatically think number one is a tremendous work ethic. It'll overcome a lot of faults and it will empower all your strengths."

Coach Vermeil's compassion for players is common knowledge in NFL circles, since he speaks openly about how deeply he cares for individual players.

BILL WALSH

"Patience. Tenacity. Passion."

Coach Walsh's patience was tested as he waited for a head coaching opportunity for seventeen years as an assistant coach. Then, his tenacity and passion were on display as the 49ers of the 1980s raised the game of football to the level of artistry. The graceful precision with which they executed their game plan was inspiring to see. It was a great oil painting in motion; Jerry Rice catching a seven-yard slant in stride, hitting a seam, and then gliding across the field for a score.

LENNY WILKENS

"Number one, you have to be honest. You have to build a trust with people, because some people don't trust because of the experiences they've had. And I think once you build that, it's easier to communicate with people.

"I think you have to be consistent. Don't say one thing and do another. I've tried to be very consistent and honest and you may not like my honesty, but you're going to know where I am on a subject. I think that allows you to communicate with people because they see that day in and day out.

"And certainly with that you have to be knowledgeable, and you get knowledge through experience."

Coach Wilkens was trusted by his peers. His honesty and integrity led him to be a player rep, and eventually vice president of the NBA Player's Association.

JOHN WOODEN

"I have as the cornerstones of my Pyramid of Success, and I think these are the most important—all are important—but the most important are industriousness and enthusiasm."

CHAPTER SIX

VIEWING FAILURE

B asketball god Michael Jordan *missed* over 16,000 shots.
Pete Rose, baseball's all-time hits leader, made more than 8,000 *outs*.

Tiger Woods, golf's greatest player, has *lost* more than 70 percent of the tournaments he has entered.

Baseball's best pitcher, Roger "The Rocket" Clemens has *lost* nearly two hundred games.

Movie star Brad Pitt made *Seven Years in Tibet.*

You have to try in order to succeed. And when you try, it's likely that you're going to fail—at least in the beginning. Michael Jordan didn't win a championship until his eighth season in the league. He then won six titles in his next six full seasons. Scotty Bowman lost his first three Stanley Cup Finals but went on to win nine of his next ten. If they had been discouraged by these early disappointments, neither Bowman nor Jordan would have achieved the sustained greatness for which they are both known.

I was an actor for a number of years in Los Angeles, and one of my favorite stars is Jack Nicholson. The Joker has become one of America's most celebrated and popular movie icons. But before Jack became a household name, he was just a journeyman actor, knocking around Hollywood for almost fifteen years. He worked as a stagehand and a character actor in B films before he finally got his big break.

In 1968, Rip Torn turned down a role in a low-budget film, opening the door of opportunity for the thirty-five-year-old Nicholson. Jack took the part. The movie was *Easy Rider,* an independent hit that catapulted Jack to superstardom. It seemed he had become a star overnight, but this culmination had actually taken more than a decade of groundwork.

The coaches' approach to failure was workmanlike also. They view failure as another step on the road to their destination. Toward the end of his interview, John Wooden added this comment, which I think encapsulates how to approach failure:

"Don't give up. Keep plugging. Know that the road to anything worthwhile is not going to be easy and it shouldn't be. There'll be obstacles along the way. You may have to change your method. You may have to back up, you may have to go around, you may have to go over, under. But don't give up. Know that good things are difficult to achieve and that's exactly the way it should be."

There are things that every one of us wants to achieve, and after completing the interviews, I'd have to agree with the coaches: The only person who really fails is the person who doesn't try.

How do you view failure?

RED AUERBACH

"Sometimes when a guy fails, it's due to an unfortunate run of luck; I understand that. But a lot of times a guy fails because he's taking shortcuts. He thinks he can fool everybody, and that everybody is more stupid than he is. He isn't willing to do the work. That's the way I look at it."

Auerbach's work ethic was formed early on. Growing up in Brooklyn, the son of a Russian immigrant father, he earned money washing the windows of taxicabs lined up waiting for gas in the 1920s and 1930s. He also worked long hours for his father, pressing suits at his dry cleaning business.

Later, as Red developed as a ballplayer, his work ethic on the court made him a gritty defensive specialist, and he was often assigned the task of shutting down the opposition's best offensive player.

DUSTY BAKER

"I think it's when you're afraid to try. When you fail, get up and try it again. Failure is when you cease to dream, when you cease to try to get better."

BRIAN BILLICK

"I think it was Churchill (and I may be getting two quotes confused), but he said 'Failure is nothing more than the opportunity to begin again more intelligently.' And the other one was 'Success is born of going from one failure to the next.'

"Those two quotes I think really define failure. Failure, like success, *you* have to determine. But I think if you are true to yourself and there are failures, as there are always going to be, then they will be less devastating to you. Because by having defined your own success, you realize that the failure really is just temporary."

Coach Billick is extremely well read and often quotes historical figures. He has authored several books:

Competitive Leadership: Twelve Principles for Success
Developing an Offensive Game Plan
Finding the Winning Edge *(coauthored with Bill Walsh)*

Henry Ford said, "Failure is only the opportunity to begin again more intelligently."

Winston Churchill said, "Success is going from failure to failure with no loss of enthusiasm."

NICK BOLLETTIERI

"Failure means to me that you're not willing to try it again. That's failure—when you give up. When something happens and you don't try it again or take a different approach, that's failure. The opportunity is there, but perhaps you just try it one time and you consider that a failure, so your concept of success and the majority of people's concept of success is too quick."

SCOTTY BOWMAN

"I don't think you're a failure if you don't enjoy what you're doing, because everybody's not going to be like that. But I think the biggest failures may be people who individually don't reach their potential. And everybody doesn't have the same potential, I realize that. So, if you reach your potential at your vocation, then you can say you're pretty successful."

As a hockey coach Bowman realized his full potential, compensating for a playing career cut short by injury.

JOHN CHANEY

"One of my great mottos that I've already had licensed is 'Be the Dream.' Don't dream, be the dream. Another is 'Winning Is an Attitude.' You win with good attitude. You get a job because you go in with a good attitude.

"You're not a failure because the score is not in your favor. You're a failure if you say to yourself that you didn't accomplish your goals, if you admit to yourself that the other guy was a winner because of the score.

"You cannot measure winning and losing by the score. There is such a thing as lo*sing* and there is such a thing as a lo*ser.* Lo*sing* is found in the score. Lo*ser* is when you internalize it to mean you. It's about your attitude."

Coach Chaney's winning attitude permeated his basketball program. His teams were considered winners for the effort they put out, and though they didn't win the NCAA championship they were respected for maximizing their ability.

BILL COWHER

"Failure? Minor setback. I think everybody at times goes through it. Failure is not fatal. It can almost be an opportunity to grow, to overcome things. You never appreciate something until you don't have it. Sometimes you may have to fail and not achieve something so it makes when you do achieve it that much greater. So to me failure is part of growth; it allows you to go to another level."

After posting winning records in Cowher's first six seasons, his teams hit some bumps in the road, finishing under .500 in 1998 and 1999. By 2001, they overcame these setbacks and returned to the NFL's elite, finishing with a 13–3 record. In 2004, Pittsburgh finished with the best regular season record in franchise history at 15–1.

ANNE DONOVAN

"Failure is when you don't do everything in your power and your control to better yourself, your team, or your organization. When you don't see the big picture—which is winning a game and not necessarily how many points you score—I think that's another time when people get off track."

After turning around the Charlotte Sting program in 2001, Coach Donovan moved on to the Seattle Storm and became the first female head coach to win a WNBA championship in 2004. She is fast asserting herself as one of the top leaders in her league.

ANGELO DUNDEE

"Failure, that's a dirty word to me. I don't ever want to fail. You try to do the right thing in life. And it doesn't make you a Goody Two-shoes if you don't fail. Failure, that's a word I don't play around with. I don't think I'm gonna fail, I don't want to fail. I want to be a winner."

Dundee's reaction is memorable to me, not so much for what he said but how he said it. He sounded like he was allergic to failure and recoiled from the word, emphatically stating his aversion to the notion of being a failure.

TONY DUNGY

"Failure to me is doing less than what you're capable of doing. I've been on some great teams that didn't win championships but got close, and didn't maybe play up to their potential all the time.

"So to me, to be able to do something, but not do it, is failure because you haven't lived up to the abilities that God has given you. The person who does what they're capable of doing, that's a success."

Coach Dungy knows how important it is to play up to your potential and how rare championship opportunities can be. An NFL veteran of nearly thirty years as both a player and coach, he has been a member of many winning teams, but won the Super Bowl just once, with the Steelers in 1979.

HERMAN EDWARDS

"Failure to me is when you quit. And when you have conflict and hard times, then all of a sudden it's easy to quit. But you have to finish. Sometimes you have to finish the race even though you're in last place. If you start something, finish it. It doesn't matter if you're in last place, go finish it. Don't quit. If you don't finish what you started, then that becomes habitually what you do. Your habits create who you are."

We continued . . .

CK: "Your determination comes across."

HE: "I always tell players, 'When you guys compete, don't worry about the other guy. You compete against yourself. It ain't about the other guy. He just happens to be in the arena, but it doesn't have anything to do with him. It's got to do with you. And that's because you can't lie to yourself. You know you could have run five more yards, you could have done two more push-ups. You know it. No one else knows it but you.'"

JEFF FISHER

"As long as you are doing everything you possibly can to reach your objective and quest, there really is no such thing as failure. If you cut corners and sell yourself short, and you can't look yourself in the eye in the mirror, then there's the potential for failure. But if you're doing everything you can to beat failure, then it's just a setback. And we can overcome setbacks."

Fisher played with nineteen-year NFL veteran Bruce Matthews at USC, and then coached him with the Titans. Matthews is familiar with Fisher's work ethic, commenting, "He's pretty much all business. As much as players talk about wanting to have the freedom to make plays on the field and not be babysat off it, you quickly realize that discipline is what wins. Jeff pays attention to the little things, because those things add up and cost you games."

DAN GABLE

"Failure to me is really just a lack of preparation. It could also be a lack of understanding, which is why you're unprepared—because you don't understand the situation. Failure occurs when you have not implemented the correct regimen to make the accomplishments. And I'm not real fond of it. [Laughs.]"

Coach Gable's workout regimen as a wrestler was legendary and he continued this practice as a coach. He maintained strict strength and conditioning workouts year-round, not just during wrestling season. He believes this prevents injuries while maintaining strength of mind, and it's hard to argue with his results.

BRAD GILBERT

"As a kid my ultimate vision of failure was the 'Agony of Defeat' on *Wide World of Sports*. But I don't like to think about it. There is no failure. There is 'You tried your ass off and it didn't go well,' [but if you lose] you pat the person on the back and get after it the next time. There is no failure. The only failure is if you didn't try. If you gave your all and you didn't win, so be it and move on."

For years, ABC's Wide World of Sports *opened with a montage that included a skier violently crashing down the side of a snowy mountain. The skier was Vinko Borgataj of Slovenia, and he actually chose to fall instead of finishing his jump. He would later say that the jumping surface was too fast and if he had continued his jump, he would have landed beyond the sloped landing area, causing potentially fatal injuries. Borgataj suffered a concussion from his crash, but is alive and well today, living in Slovenia.*

CARRIE GRAF

"To me, failure is the inability to handle adversity. Mistakes are a part of life, and how you respond to them decides whether you're a success or a failure.

"If you can bounce back from an error or mistake, that's the trait that successful people have. People that falter—have a mistake, have a failure—and can't overcome that, that's when it becomes a failure."

APRIL HEINRICHS

"My first instinct is to say it's something I haven't experienced often in my life. It's infuriating when I do. I guess when failure occurs in my life I self-evaluate beyond a reasonable amount of time and a reasonable amount of opportunity. It is devastating to feel and I do everything I can to not feel that at all costs; hence the work ethic.

"But you always learn something from failing. Because I don't care who you are and how ambitious you are—when you fail, you self-evaluate more critically. And you look internally for the responsibilities; at least I do, for the accountability and where the plan may have slipped up. When you fail you look far more critically at your accountability and your level of responsibility.

"When you have success—and I think it's very human in nature—without some checks and balances, you don't critically analyze as much. I think self-evaluation skills are one of the most important skills in life: the ability to check yourself, to check how you're doing as a human being. Are you a good citizen? Are you where you want to be? Do people have the same perception of you that you have of yourself? And if not, how can you self-correct? How can you become a better person each year or a better professional or a better loved one?

"So, failure in anything forces you to self-evaluate in ways many people don't do regularly. Avoid it at all costs, but analyze it when it happens! [Laughs.]"

Heinrichs has always been a winner—in college, the pros, and internationally. When she took over coaching the U.S. team she caught some criticism for the team's losses at the Olympics in 2000 and the FIFA Women's World Cup USA in 2003. But Heinrichs and the team persisted and broke through in 2004, winning the Olympic gold medal.

WHITEY HERZOG

"I never, ever thought about failing. You have to have extreme confidence in yourself to be successful, and you have to know that what you're doing is the right way and never look back.

"I don't know, but failure might be not giving 100 percent. Failure might be that you didn't work as hard at something as you should have, that you might have gone about it halfheartedly. You don't realize the success you could have if you put more effort into it."

KEN HITCHCOCK

"As a coach it's not getting your team to make sacrifices for each other. I feel like that's failing to get the job done. Your job as a coach in our business is to get the players to do very uncomfortable tasks and then learn to enjoy those tasks. And when a coach is unable to get his team to do that, he's failed."

No one questions the dedication of Coach Hitchcock's teams. In 2004, the Flyers took eventual champion Tampa Bay to seven games before losing in the Eastern Conference Finals. Hitchcock's Dallas Stars took the New Jersey Devils to six games in 2000, before losing the Stanley Cup in double overtime.

BELA KAROLYI

"Failing is just as natural as succeeding. There is only one first place. But failing at a particular moment needs to be taken as an incentive to succeed next time. If it is not understood this way, it is extremely, extremely detrimental.

"My greatest fights with my athletes were always after an unfulfilled expectation of a major competition. I would say, 'We are not losers. We did not lose at all. We failed to complete our goal, but that is the incentive to go for next time.'

"Failure is not losing. We are not losers. Failing to complete your expectations is not losing at all."

Many of Karolyi's gymnasts are young enough that they need the encouragement he offers to continue to strive toward their goals. He is always seen encouraging his athletes after they have poor performances.

TRUDI LACEY

"Failure is when you allow it to stop you from trying again. Failure is not final, it's just a temporary setback. It's not what happens to you, it's how you handle it, in every experience. No matter if you have a successful experience or if you don't get the result that you want, every experience that you have is a learning experience. And if you look at every experience that you have as a learning experience, there is no such thing as failure."

MARVIN LEWIS

"A lack of preparation."

One of the first things Coach Lewis did as head coach of the Bengals was to rip out the old weight room and request a $250,000 renovation. He immediately hired new strength and conditioning coaches, and instituted off-season training and diet programs in order to improve players' strength, stamina, and overall health.

Lewis was only with the Bengals for three years in 2005, but the changes he made had a noticeable difference as the Bengals have now become one of the league's best teams.

TOM OSBORNE

"I think failure is essentially not being true to the gifts you've been given. In other words, if you have abilities and talents and you don't use them or if you squander opportunities, to me that's failure. Being less than you're capable of. And nobody completely measures up; there's always some element of missing the mark in all of us.

"But generally speaking there are some people who use what they've been given to a high degree and then there are those who really squander some tremendous talents. And that was always the most heartbreaking thing to me—to see a player who had been given so much in terms of ability and sometimes intelligence, and to see them throw it all away and not realize it."

A prime example of what he's talking about is the abundantly talented running back Lawrence Phillips. In 1996, Osborne was harshly criticized for reinstating Phillips onto Nebraska's national championship team after Phillips had been suspended for assaulting his girlfriend. Although he was loaded with ability, Phillips never realized his promise. He's had numerous run-ins with the law and continues to struggle with personal demons.

BILL PARCELLS

"Failure is a word that is only truthful when someone's willing to accept it. I just feel like there's a way out no matter how far down and out you are. No matter what the perception of you is, no matter what's happened in your life, until you just give up, there's a way out.

"Failure can only be final if a person gives in to it, accepts it. You can alter your circumstances no matter how bad they seem to be."

This strength of will is a Parcells trademark and one of his greatest assets. He instills his teams with his own belief in himself, and is known as one of football's greatest psychologists.

MIKE SCIOSCIA

"I think that failure stems from lack of effort.

"If someone goes through college and is trying to get a degree and they fall short—their grades just don't match up—and they studied and did as well as they could and reached a certain level academically, and it happened to be an associate's degree instead of a bachelor's degree, hey, I don't think that's a failure. Or if someone gets a bachelor's degree and is going for a master's and just can't get it done. Or an attorney who goes through law school and just has trouble passing the bar. I don't look at that as failure if the effort was there and they took the steps along the way and just could not get over that last hurdle because their talent wouldn't let them. That's not a failure.

"A failure is someone who can achieve but takes the other road for whatever reason. It goes back to the idea that it's better to have played the game and lost than to not have played at all."

Scioscia gleaned his commonsense approach growing up in Upper Darby, Pennsylvania, a middle-class suburb of Philadelphia, and from his longtime manager with the Los Angeles Dodgers, Tommy Lasorda, another Philadelphia-area native, who grew up in Norristown, Pennsylvania.

TUBBY SMITH

"You might get a failing grade, but that doesn't mean that you're a failure. You might lose the game, but that doesn't mean you're a loser. A failure is a person who cannot overcome their bad habits and bad behavior. Everybody should be able to change; it's what life is all about. But if you can't change your behavior and your attitude, then I think you're a failure in that regard.

"You should be able to change once you realize 'I was wrong here,' or 'I was addicted to this.' If you can't change and if you don't change then you're a failure. If you keep doing it over and over again and everybody's there to help you and all you've got to do is change, it may not be easy, but if you don't then you failed."

Coach Smith learned the discipline needed to overcome bad habits from his father, Guffrie Smith, who worked three jobs while raising his family: He drove a school bus, fired boilers at a naval air station, and barbered.

EMANUEL STEWARD

"When a person has accepted that he's failed and gives up, that to me is really failure. A lot of times failure can be just temporary, like detours on a trip. You have to get off the road, maybe go a little bit out of the way, but you get back on track and you keep going. But once you accept that you're not going to make it to your destination and you give up, that's failure.

"And you have to learn to be able to reconstruct yourself. You have to say, 'What I'm doing is not working, is not compatible with who I am, so let me try this a different way.' That's the difference. You have to make adjustments and redirect your priorities sometimes."

Steward reconstructed himself several times. Before becoming one of America's greatest boxing trainers, he worked as an electrician, a cosmetics salesman, and an event promoter.

JOE TORRE

"Failure is such a tough word because the only way you can ever learn how to win is to know what it feels like to lose. Failure is something that you have to put behind you in a hurry.

"In 2004, we lost to the Red Sox in four straight games after we had them down three games to none and were one inning away from going to the World Series. As a manager, I can look at it differently than a player. As a player I used to beat myself up because I felt I was personally responsible for not winning in many instances, and that was really unfair to myself.

"But as a manager, I look at the preparation and the effort of my players and how passionate they were and how hurt they are when you come up short. And to me, failure is just a learning tool, and that's the way you need to look at it. You just have to learn from whatever events go on in your life and move on.

"That was tough for me when I first started managing. I used to really beat myself up for managerial decisions I made when I didn't have as talented a club as I do now. I realize now that instead of kicking yourself about doing something, you're better off saying the next time this circumstance presents itself you'll learn from the last time you did it."

CK: "And as far as the Red Sox thing, sometimes it just happens."

JT: "Yes, sometimes it just happens. The thing that some people don't realize is that the year before we were down four runs in the middle of the game with Pedro Martinez on the mound. I mean what was the likelihood of us winning that game? You can't only think of me, me, me. After Game 7 was over and we lost, I thought of Tim Wakefield the year before, who had pitched wonderfully against us, and who gave up a home run on one pitch and to watch him walk off the field. . . . And for everyone to characterize that as a failure, it wasn't fair. It wasn't fair. Unfortunately, in our line of work and in society it's all about beating people up and blaming people. I mean, we had the blackout in New York a few years ago and instead of trying to find the mechanism to make sure it won't happen again, we keep trying to find the one person who's responsible so we can beat him up."

CK: "Bill Buckner."

JT: "Right."

CK: "That guy was one of the best hitters I ever saw."

JT: "[He was one of the] best hitters and that game was tied at the time and the momentum had already switched and to drop that thing on him was ridiculous, but that's what we are. Donnie Moore in that same year. He gave up the home run, but the Angels came back and tied the game and had the winning run at third base with one out, but couldn't score it. But that's where we are.

"Failure's someplace where you don't hang pictures, you move on."

In 2004, after eighty-six years without winning a World Series, the Boston Red Sox defeated their longtime tormentors, the New York Yankees, four games to three, after losing the first three games of the American League Championship Series. They then went on to sweep the St. Louis Cardinals and win the World Series.

The next season, when the Yankees visited Boston's Fenway Park, the Red Sox held a ceremony to give World Series rings to their players. To honor the Red Sox, the Yankees came out of their dugout and gave the Boston players a standing ovation as they received their rings. This classy move is credited to Torre and is an excellent example of how he runs his team.

In 1986, Donnie Moore, the California Angels' closer, gave up a game-winning home run in the ALCS to Dave Henderson, which turned the series around—the Boston Red Sox eventually won. Moore's career never recovered, and he committed suicide in 1989.

JOHN TORTORELLA

"Failure is allowing the process to beat you. That's the way I look at it. Anyone who wants to be successful doesn't say, 'OK, next week—today is Monday, on Sunday I'm gonna be successful at this.' There's always a process [that takes] a tremendous amount of time to be successful. I think failure is allowing that process, allowing some of the adversities, to get at you and keep you from attaining your goals."

He expanded on getting through the process . . .

CK: "You mean when the system beats you?"

JT: "Yeah, when the process beats you. And sometimes failing, within a certain time period, is still part of the process to get to your goal. Sometimes you need to lose to understand what it is to win, what it takes to be successful. So that is still within the process—it's allowing that certain failure or that certain loss to eat you up and not allow you to continue trying to go through the process.

   "That's an important note because you have to learn some of the things that went bad in certain situations in order to continue to grow and to try to be successful. The failure is when you say, 'I just quit. OK, I failed; I quit. I'm not going to bother trying to go through the process anymore.' That's what I consider failure."

DICK VERMEIL

"I think first it's a breakdown in your moral structure, a breakdown in your relationships with people close to you. And then it's a breakdown in the responsibilities that you have in your profession."

BILL WALSH

"It's when you concede and begin to give up. When you lose your focus on what you're doing and then you just go through the motions attempting it—that's failure."

As coach of the San Francisco 49ers, Coach Walsh didn't go through the motions. He took an ordinary offense and elevated it to an art form.

LENNY WILKENS

"[Laughs.] You know, there's an old saying, 'Failure is just a chance to try again.' That's how we look at it. I tell my players, 'You've got to risk failure to be successful.' You can't be afraid to take a shot because you might miss. You can't play to keep from losing, because you're going to lose if you do.

"If you don't succeed one way, then reevaluate and find out what you can do differently. 'Am I going in the right direction? Is this the right way to do this?' Do a little self-analysis and start over, but don't quit."

Coach Wilkens isn't afraid to lose. In fact, he has both won more games and lost more games than any other coach in NBA history.

JOHN WOODEN

"There is no such thing as failure to the person who makes the effort to do the best they could do. It's like character and reputation. You're the only one that knows your character. Your reputation is what others perceive you to be. Character is far more important. For example, I think you can be successful and be outscored in a game. I think you can be unsuccessful when you outscore an opponent.

"You know, it's sort of like my definition of success; it's peace of mind, and without peace of mind, I don't think we have much."

Coach Wooden's reputation stems from his character. He is recognized as one of the top all-time coaches in American sports history, along with Vince Lombardi and Knute Rockne.

CHAPTER SEVEN

RELATING MONEY TO SUCCESS

When I was younger I thought success was all about money. Now I know better.

The neighborhood I grew up in reminds people of the movies *A Bronx Tale* and *Goodfellas*—lots of Cadillacs and Lincoln Continentals cruising around. And although most south Philadelphians are decent, hardworking, and honest (sometimes brutally so), there's also a criminal element that's easy to spot.

The gangsters always had the nicest cars, designer clothes, and flashed the most cash. A person could easily get the wrong impression as to whether or not crime pays.

Luckily for me, my older brother moved out to Los Angeles when I was twenty years old and I followed him a couple of months later. This change of scenery opened up new horizons for me. I was exposed to art and theater, and people from all over the world. Then I became involved in acting and writing, and my life changed for the better.

As I pursued a career in show business, my friends back East followed their own paths. Some got married and took regular jobs. Others went to college to become professionals. And another crew went for the fast money through whatever means they knew. Now that over twenty years have passed, the results of these choices are crystal clear. The family men are doing fine. The professionals are also doing well. But most of the guys who went for the fast money have lives in disarray. This is in spite of the fact that they made more money than anybody.

My point is that money without a foundation can be a formula for disaster. One of the reasons I wrote this book is because kids watch

MTV's *Cribs* and *Fabulous Lifestyles of Hollywood Celebrities* and want what stars have, but they have no idea of what it takes to get those things. I'm not an old fogy. I don't think kids are bad and only want money. I think some kids can be easily influenced, especially by television and movies (I know I was), and need to be shown that money isn't the answer; it's one of the rewards of hard work.

Bill Parcells's comment about money sums it up best for me. He tells his players that pro football will give them wealth and fame, but it won't give them championships; they have to earn them. The same goes for a good life—money won't give you that, you have to earn it.

How would you relate money to success?

RED AUERBACH

"Well, how I would relate it is different from the way most people do. To me, success is being the best you can be at your craft. To me a guy who's a great cabinetmaker or a great carpenter or a great teacher, he's as great as a guy who plunked down $5,000 on a stock and it went through the roof and he became a millionaire.

"I have more respect for a guy who's the best at what he does. I don't care if he's an artist or what he does. As long as he achieved as close to excellence as he could."

In 1980, the Professional Basketball Writers Association of America recognized Auerbach's excellence when they named him the greatest coach in the history of the NBA.

DUSTY BAKER

"I think our country relates it to success a lot. But there are a lot of artists, entertainers, and people that died broke whose talents weren't realized until years later. If you leave something lasting—a positive, lasting impression during or after your duration for future generations, then I think you're a success."

Dusty Baker keeps in touch with the next generation through his work with various youth organizations, such as Willie Mays's Say Hey Foundation and United Way.

BRIAN BILLICK

"Study after study after study tells you that monetary return rarely if ever is a true motivator. That's a bit naive. Certainly there are things that money can bring you that are attractive enough to drive you. But I would agree that if that is your ultimate goal, you're on a path where eventually you're gonna find that ultimately money is not what's gonna make you happy—and therefore you're not successful. Because that's too easily won and lost."

Coach Billick talked about his experience with wealthy people . . .

"Having been at a place like Stanford, being in this game and interacting with a lot of brilliant and rich people, there are still some men I know who in a New York second would trade places with me, even though they make ten times as much as I do. Because of the conviction and passion that this game requires, they admire that. That has taught me a lot, interacting with those types of people who have all the money in the world. So you have to realize that this isn't going to sustain me beyond just the fact that I made a lot of money."

NICK BOLLETTIERI

"I'd rather use something Arthur Ashe told me one time: 'Nick, self-satisfaction is the greatest reward of life. That you know you did it. Not the world. You know you did it.' And that to me is not measured in dollars. That is measured when you know you've done something good for an inner city. It's not publicized in the paper, but you've affected the lives of many thousands of children. And that reward is far greater than becoming a multimillionaire."

Arthur Ashe was a prominent African American tennis player known for his efforts to further social causes. He is the only black man to win singles titles at Wimbledon, the Australian Open, and the U.S. Open.

BOBBY BOWDEN

"Money would be the secular way of saying you're successful. But I've known people who had all the money in the world who committed suicide. So it must not be the answer. It depends on what you do with money. Let's say a guy becomes a millionaire. If he's stingy with it and buys everything for himself and nobody else, he's not doing right. Now, if he takes that money and gives to charity, gives to his church, gives to the poor—then that's money relating to success. Do good with money. Share it."

SCOTTY BOWMAN

"Well, that's not always something that happens. There are a lot of successful people that you can't relate money to. They enjoy doing what they're doing and I think that is what being successful comes down to.

"Looking at sports, if a guy's a hotshot player in any sport he's probably not going to have much money worries."

CK:　"But to the average Joe?"

SB:　"I think for the average Joe, a lot of people look at money and think it's the answer, but sometimes it isn't."

Bowman has coached several generations of the NHL's hotshot players, including Steve Yzerman, Sergei Federov, Mario Lemieux, Dominik Hasek, and Guy Lafleur. In 2004, the NHL's average salary was approximately $1.5 million.

JOHN CHANEY

"Oh my God, that's a big one. That's one of the competing things that we find. I look at TV and see a thirteen-year-old girl playing in the LPGA, like she's outta sight."

CK:　"Michelle Wie."

JC:　"Yes. And all of these tennis players that are earning millions of dollars at fifteen and sixteen years old and retiring at twenty-two. Althea Gibson was in her thirties, I think, when she won Wimbledon, so she was an old woman according to today's standards. These kids retire at twenty-two.

"But here's what puzzles me—this young girl who golfs, they're bragging about how great she is, how wonderful she is, how great she's going to be. She's beautiful, she's terrific— they're using all kinds of positive adjectives to describe her, yet we find on the other hand that people are suggesting that an eighteen-year-old, nineteen-year-old, or twenty-year-old high school basketball player that somebody offers millions of dollars to isn't ready yet, that he should go to college!

"You tell me, this kid LeBron James, who just got $90 million from Nike, didn't go to college. We find people who are expressing their morality to these youngsters. Now here's the other point—does race matter, since basketball is inhabited by 80 percent blacks? And the privileged sports like golf and tennis are inhabited by 90 percent whites? Does race intervene? Does it find itself raising its ugly head when black kids coming out of basketball go out and don't go to college? Kobe Bryant and all these guys—there's about twenty of them that didn't go to college that ended up with millions of dollars now in the NBA. Kevin Garnett is the highest-paid player in the NBA, he didn't go to college. Tracy McGrady, Darius Miles, Rashard Lewis, Jermaine O'Neal; I'm talking about guys that are all millionaires and doing well. What did money have to do to influence them? You can't go up and tell those kids that I want you to go to college when somebody's offering them a million dollars, and express your morality about that, and not express the fact that this woman is playing in the LPGA. She should not be out there at thirteen years old.

"My point is money makes a big difference, especially when some pious person comes up and suggests to a youngster that this is what you should do. Like the NCAA, perhaps the worst ad hoc committee in the history of sports, who has more don'ts in it than dos, always in the name of the integrity of the sport. And yet these youngsters are able to look out their window and say, 'Hey, wait a minute, you're telling me that I shouldn't accept this million dollars, and yet you are accepting money for what you're doing. Or, I look out my window and see the other kids of another race accepting millions of dollars at an earlier age than me.' So, the kid says, 'Well, why can't I? Why shouldn't I take advantage of this?'

"And then we look at the other demographic that we have to deal with and that is the fact that we have 60 to 70 percent of all of our black kids with one-parent families or less. And it's growing. When you look at the NBA draft, every time they call a black kid up, who was there? The mother, no father. LeBron

James, just keep on going down the line. There was no father. So we're looking at youngsters whose lives are being shaped by economics, or lack of economics. Many of these fathers, when they don't have an education, they don't have a good job, they're not making money to support a family. They *run* away from the responsibility!"

Coach Chaney is an outspoken voice in the black community. Here he refers to what he views as a double standard concerning how young black men in the NBA get scrutinized for their financial and educational choices, where as nonblacks in tennis, golf, and other sports do not. He has a point that despite widespread criticism, most of the basketball players who have skipped college and gone directly to the NBA have been quite successful.

BILL COWHER

"I think it's a measuring tool, but I'm not so sure that it truly can define someone's success. Maybe you can measure their success, but I don't think you can define it because I don't think success should be defined by how much they make. Success should be defined by one's contribution to others' development and one's own happiness. I don't think people that are unhappy, even though they make a lot of money are successful.

"Money is more of a measuring tool that our society has put on people. Unfortunately, at times I think we misjudge the whole element of what successful people should be made of."

Steelers ownership didn't misjudge Cowher's ability back in 2001. After missing the playoffs in three consecutive seasons, owner Dan Rooney gave Cowher a contract extension. He cited the coach's quality personality as one of the main reasons to extend his contract—in spite of the disappointing seasons. Cowher has since restored the Steelers to greatness.

ANNE DONOVAN

"Money can be a result of success, but not always. And to me that's the cherry on the cake. If that comes with success, that's the cherry. The process—the feeling good about what you do on a day-to-day basis—is the icing. The financial gain is the cherry."

In 2005, the salary cap in the WNBA was set at $647,000 per team because of financial constraints, thereby limiting the financial gain of female players. In 2002, Donovan said, "I don't know how many coaches in this league are getting rich, but if that's being put out there, it's a fallacy."

TONY DUNGY

"Not very much at all. I don't equate money with success because there are a lot of ways to make money and some of them aren't going to make you a very successful person in life. And then some of the greatest undertakings that one could go after and achieve will have involved very little monetary reward. That's one of the things that Chuck Knoll taught me when I first started working—don't make any decisions based on money. And I didn't list that as the best advice I ever got, but it's right up there."

Chuck Knoll was head coach of the Pittsburgh Steelers from 1969 to 1991. He guided them to four Super Bowl wins, in 1975, 1976, 1979, and 1980. He was elected to the Pro Football Hall of Fame in 1993.

HERMAN EDWARDS

"In this way—it's only good if you give it back."

Edwards received the Big Brother of the Year Award from the Catholic Big Brothers for Boys and Girls in 2002, and has hosted the Herman Edwards Football Camp for underprivileged children in Monterey since 1996.

JEFF FISHER

"I really don't believe that the two are related. One is a by-product of the other, but that's the only way they're related. There are many, many successful people that are the best at what they do, that don't do it for financial reasons. And there aren't always financial rewards there. It really depends on what you do, but money is a by-product of success. You have to be successful first in order to achieve the wealth, if in fact that is a priority or goal of yours. But money is overrated."

Midway through the 1999 season, Fisher was given a "make the play-offs or you're fired" mandate from owner Bud Adams. The Titans produced, made it to the Super Bowl, and Fisher was then rewarded with a contract extension and a hefty raise.

DAN GABLE

"Money shouldn't be the motivating factor that drives you into doing something, but when you're doing something right, and for the right reasons, then money usually isn't a major problem.

"My athletic director, when I first went to work at Iowa, told me, 'Come see me after every season, and based on your performance, if you have a good year, we'll do a little for you.' Instead of saying he was going to give me a million dollars upfront to perform—you do something, you make accomplishments, and you are rewarded."

Gable's performance earned him a twenty-one-year tenure as head coach of Iowa's wrestling team and he remains employed by the university as assistant to the director of athletics in charge of performance enhancement.

BRAD GILBERT

"I guess money is nice, it gives you the perks . . . but money can make you an asshole.

"Money doesn't make the person. It's a by-product of what you do. If you have a good upbringing and a good background and everything like that, I think about the person before I think about money. The most important thing about money is that you can take care of your family."

CARRIE GRAF

"I don't think that's how you should measure success. There are a lot of people who are successful in what they do and they're not living in huge mansions, they're not driving fancy cars. They're successful because they've had a successful and enjoyable life.

"And particularly if it's someone involved in women's sports, often we don't make a huge amount of money. It's not about the money, it's about being pioneers and working toward something and hoping for the day that we can be on some sort of a par, but thinking that money equals success—you're barking up the wrong tree."

CK: "It must be an interesting thing from your perspective to see the men making all this money and the women are more or less still in the infancy stage of your league."

CG: "Yeah, and not just the female thing. It astounds me the way some industries overpay certain skills. In education, teachers are still not a highly paid profession in Australia as well as the United States, and I think that teachers should be one of the highest-paid professions."

In 2004, the maximum salary for a WNBA player was $90,000. Comparatively, the minimum salary for an NBA rookie is more than quadruple that amount, at around $385,000.

Many WNBA players supplement their salaries by playing in European leagues in the off-season.

APRIL HEINRICHS

"It's nice, it's really nice. [Laughs.]"

CK: "I like your honesty."

AH: "Yeah, it's really nice. Money would never keep me from choosing a job, taking a job, or it would never entice me to take a job I wouldn't want. Money really doesn't matter to me when it comes to what I want. When it comes to a profession or a career or a direction, I could be doing exactly what I'm doing and if I got paid so many thousand dollars a year I'd be just fine. I would never stay in a position longer than I would enjoy it because the money was good.

"I've met a couple of women who are in the business world who are making $200,000 a year and I am just . . . my level of respect for them unequivocally escalates. Because it's hard for a young woman—thirty-something, forty-something—

to be making that kind of money. They've obviously done extremely well and they're being compensated for it.

"On the other hand, we all know that you could have all the money in the world and it doesn't make you a happy person. It certainly makes some of life's stresses easier to accept, but I think beyond a reasonable amount of income per year, money is a neutralizing thing in my life. As long as I can pay the rent, have a car, do the things I want to do—and I live pretty meagerly—then beyond that I could care less about money."

The U.S. women's soccer team successfully boycotted several games in 2000, demanding that their salaries be increased to be on a par with the men's team. The women's salaries were increased; however, most observers believe they are still underpaid.

WHITEY HERZOG

"Money comes after success, unless you're born with a silver spoon in your mouth. That's the only time you would have money ahead of time.

"I've been fortunate. I've always said that baseball's been very good to me, especially after I quit trying to play. Once I became a manager and had success in Kansas City and St. Louis, the money started to come my way. I don't really think that money makes you successful. I think that once you have success, then the money takes care of itself."

After retiring as a player, Herzog flourished as a manager, winning six division titles, three pennants, and one World Series championship.

KEN HITCHCOCK

"You're gonna find this very strange—I really wish that I lived in a time where money was not a factor. I wish that I lived in a time where you could barter and trade for everything. I don't really focus on the money. I've never been one that concerns myself with the country club that I'm a member at or how big my car is. I want to be comfortable, but I also feel that money becomes a huge hindrance.

"In our sport it isn't the best players that win, it's the best team. And it's not related to how much money you make."

BELA KAROLYI

"Nowadays money has become very closely related to success. Most of the time athletes and the most successful people are rewarded with money. It's very unfortunate, very unfortunate. I never considered this as a number-one criterion for success. And if money is all you think about in becoming a successful person, then you are a failure already.

"The monetary reward will come, but only after you complete the grueling experience that makes you successful."

In order to reap the financial benefits of being the world's foremost gymnastics coach, Coach Karolyi first had to defect from communist Romania—where he received little to no monetary compensation for his efforts—to the United States.

TRUDI LACEY

"I don't believe that money defines you. I think that you have to be a successful person first on the inside. No matter your title, no matter how much money you make, no matter the house that you live in.

Because if you define your success by a paycheck, what happens to you when you no longer have that? You feel like a nobody.

"The one great thing about having money is that you can use that money to help people that are less fortunate than yourself. It's like the quote 'To whom much is given, much is expected.' It's not the amount of money that you have, it's how you use that money and what good can be done with that money."

Coach Lacey helps people in her community, actively supporting a number of nonprofit organizations such as the Girl Scouts, Samaritan Purse, and the Tri-County Animal Rescue.

MARVIN LEWIS

"I don't think it has anything to do with it. If you're money-oriented then you're probably gonna have a difficult time having success—if that's why you're looking for success."

In 2003, Coach Lewis and his wife, Peggy, formed the Marvin Lewis Community Fund, a nonprofit organization that raises funds to improve the lives of inner-city children in the Cincinnati area.

LUTE OLSON

"I think that's the biggest mistake some people make. They choose something to do because of the money that's going to be involved. When I started coaching, I taught six classes and was the assistant football coach, the head basketball coach, and the head baseball coach. I made $3,200. The money was never a factor, other than obviously you have to provide for your family. But I did what I did because I had a passion for it and it didn't feel like work. I enjoyed doing what I was doing and the reason I'm still doing it is because I still have that passion for it."

Olson began his career in the late 1950s, where he taught and coached at high schools in Minnesota and California for eleven years.

TOM OSBORNE

"My earlier comments would indicate some concern with the general tendency today to say that successful people are people who are wealthy, when many times you can point out people who have a lot of money who really are not very admirable people—people who do not display sound character. That is one of the main concerns that I have with our culture today. It's just the fact that we have become tremendously materialistic.

"Certainly there is nothing wrong with money. Money can be used to accomplish some great ends, but when wealth becomes its own reward and its own goal then I think it can be very destructive. Sometimes in professional athletics today or in coaching, you see people who are very disappointed or who are holding out because they aren't the highest-paid player, the highest-paid shortstop, the highest-paid coach, or whatever.

"And really, at the level that they are, the extra $100,000 or $50,000 or whatever it may be is relatively meaningless—it's all about ego. Being the highest paid, that means they're successful. I think when it gets to that point, many times it's a little bit pathological and not very healthy."

After winning three national collegiate championships, Coach Osborne did not jump to the NFL and its hefty salaries. He chose instead to move into public service and became a U.S. congressman.

BILL PARCELLS

"Money's a very relative thing. It's a tool for me; it's a vehicle for comfort. It's not anything that I deem to be on a par with achievements. I don't think that it's relative to achievement. Now, I know that a lot of people feel like it is, but I don't. I don't think it's a real reflection of anything to do with success.

"I talk to my teams a lot about it. I say, 'This game can give you a lot of comforts. It can make you famous, it can make you wealthy. But it can't give you championships. It can't give you the pinnacle. You have to earn that.' It's much different on that front because there's a certain commitment that's involved to do those things.

"And I know a lot of people that are wealthy, but only by good fortune. Some of them got lucky, some of them inherited it, you know. Some of them hit the lottery. Does that make that guy successful?"

As one of the league's highest-paid and most-accomplished coaches, Parcells has the credentials and gumption to challenge many of today's highly paid players.

MIKE SCIOSCIA

"I don't think there's any correlation at all. There are some people that are successful that have money; there are people that are successful that don't have money. And probably the most shining example of that is somebody like Mother Teresa. How could you call her life and what she did not a success? She didn't have any wealth."

"You know, my mom taught first grade for forty years. She never achieved great wealth and she worked hard because she had a passion to teach and she loved it. And her life is one of the most incredible success stories I've ever come across."

We discussed societal views on success . . .

CK: "Well, I mean we live more or less in the MTV generation where everything is about big gold chains, so sometimes it's interesting what is considered successful."

MS: "Big gold chains are great if someone wants to buy them. [Laughs.] I don't see anything wrong with that, but I don't think that wealth is any kind of measure of success in any degree.

"Maybe there are job descriptions where the wealth you create, if you're a stockbroker or an investment banker or whatever, you're going to have guidelines along those lines, but if you look around and try to make any correlation between wealth and success, I don't think it's a common denominator. I know people that have been incredibly successful in their lives and have had the fulfillment that not many people have had because they had a passion to do something. It just happened to be that what they did wasn't a great wealth producer.

"So I don't see the correlation; in fact, I think if you look at the vast majority of what I would consider successful people, they don't have incredible wealth because of their success. Some of us have the opportunity because of what we have a passion for, and what we wanted to do is very lucrative, but like I said with the examples of Mother Teresa and my mom the schoolteacher, or whatever professions there are that aren't as lucrative as others—those people that have a passion and achieve in those professions are every bit as much a success story as someone who's had the opportunity to do something that's more lucrative."

TUBBY SMITH

"Growing up in the household that I did, I understood how to value a dollar, but I also learned that if you don't have it you're still going to survive. You've got to find a way to survive.

"I didn't grow up in an environment where it was a ghetto area. I grew up where I'd go out and get in the garden or make preserves or jelly, or pick blackberries, and a lot of people don't have that, don't have access to that. All they know is going to the grocery store.

"So my contention is that money doesn't bring you happiness, doesn't bring you success, but it is a by-product of being successful. If you are doing your job and performing your services, you become more marketable. If I do a good job as an assistant coach at Kentucky, I might get a head coaching job. If I do a good job at Tulsa, then the people at Georgia are going to be impressed. If you let money be the reason you're doing things, then you're not successful in my mind."

Tubby Smith's survival skills were nurtured on his family's farm in southern Maryland, far from the media spotlight that now follows him and his Kentucky basketball team.

EMANUEL STEWARD

"Don't look at the money as much as trying to be the best that you can be. Set your goals to where you want to be the tops in that profession and then the money usually comes. It's good to be in something where you love what you do and it's not just a job. Most supersuccess stories are based on people being involved in something that they are totally in love with."

Steward stuck with his childhood love of boxing and later on moonlighted as a boxing trainer while working as an electrician to make ends meet. Eventually, his skill as a trainer developed, and his Kronk Gym became one of the world's most successful gyms, making Emanuel a supersuccess.

JOE TORRE

"It's misleading in our game nowadays. You used to be able to characterize a superstar by how much money he made. You know, he made $100,000. But now players are paid on what you hope they can give you. They used to be paid on what they did give you. So the person who thinks that because of how much money he or she makes, it makes them a success, is delusional. There's more to success than how much money you make. With that type of stuff there's a certain amount of luck involved."

Torre manages the team with the highest payroll in all of sports. In 2005, the Yankees payroll was nearly $206 million, and third baseman Alex Rodriguez is Major League Baseball's highest-paid player at nearly $26 million per year.

JOHN TORTORELLA

"I'm not a big believer that money is a measure of success. I'm talking as a coach and I want to try to answer it in an everyday situation. Sometimes that's what people think success is—money. They want to make as much money as they can. And if that's your goal to be successful, to make as much money as you can, then that has to equate to success. But I don't consider that being successful.

"I think being the best person you can be, and having the foundation of trying to be the best person you can be, is the key. The money and all that comes later on. You always reap the benefit if you decide on what type of person you want to be. That's what you need to work at—grounding yourself, finding a foundation of what you need to be as a person, as a coach, as a team, and the other stuff comes after it. So I don't think money is a big part of it. I think it will be a part of it, if you learn how to be successful."

Coach Tortorella became one of the league's best-paid coaches by working his way from the bottom to the top. He won league titles at each level he coached: with Virginia of the ACHL in 1986–87, Rochester of the AHL in 1995–96, and finally, the Stanley Cup with Tampa Bay of the NHL in 2004.

DICK VERMEIL

"It's more of a reward and a symbol of accomplishments. It's a temporary motivator. The true passion to excel is not ignited by money. It's a source of motivation, but I don't think it's the main source."

After Coach Vermeil retired from coaching in 1982, he was offered a number of lucrative deals to return to coaching. He declined until 1997, when he took over as head coach of the St. Louis Rams.

BILL WALSH

"I think that the men playing today, even those that are very mercenary with the agents and millions of dollars, still play the game because they love it. So I think if you thoroughly thrive on the activity—the game that you play—then you somehow survive to be able to play it.

"It wasn't too many years ago that professional football players had to have summer jobs in order to survive. But they played just as hard or even more fiercely than today's players, because they loved the game and thrived on the competition."

CK: "Some people just seem to be successful no matter what they're doing, even just walking down the street."

BW: "It's how you appear. If you appear slovenly then you'll think of yourself that way. I don't think people ought to dress in high fashion, but I think about Jerry Rice standing in front of the mirror before the game. He wanted his uniform to be perfect. That's what I think about people going about their daily lives and in their workplace."

Jerry Rice is generally considered the NFL's greatest all-time wide receiver. He holds virtually every significant receiving record, including touchdowns (197), receptions (1,549), and receiving yards (22,895).

LENNY WILKENS

"Money is a means to an end for a lot of people, but I don't measure money as the pinnacle of success because some people get put in a position where they can't help but make a lot of money. Athletes sometimes get paid more than they're worth because the timing is right, so I never let money color my thinking into meaning you are a success.

"You're a success if you are doing something productive, if you can influence other people's lives in a positive way, if you're giving back to your community, and you're functioning as a worthwhile person in society. That's success, not the dollar amount you have."

Coach Wilkens's career as a player and coach spanned five decades. In 1960, when he entered the league, the NBA's highest paid player was Bob Cousy at $22,500. In 2005, Shaquille O'Neal was the league's highest-paid player with a salary close to $28 million, and the average NBA salary was approximately $3.8 million.

JOHN WOODEN

"I do not relate money to success any more than I do scores to success. Other people do but I don't.

"Scores are a by-product of the effort you make to come close to your own ability. I think the same thing as far as money is concerned. [Even in] some of the professions that could lead toward making a lot of money, if [people] don't follow the cornerstones of success, they won't do it. I've often said, and maybe I've heard it somewhere, that happiness comes from the things that can't be taken away from you. And all material things can be taken away."

Wooden's modest lifestyle is a reflection of his values. Though he was one of the most influential coaches of the twentieth century, he has long lived in a modest condominium in Encino, California.

CHAPTER EIGHT

THE BEST DAYS

So many great teams and players have played under the coaches in this book. They've produced hundreds of championship moments in front of billions of people. From Super Bowls to Stanley Cups, from heavyweight championships to Olympic golds, watching these great sporting events on television was awesome, but then discussing them with the coaches during our interviews took it to another level for me.

Overall, it was inspirational to hear the pride the coaches had in achieving their dreams: when Joe Torre finally won the World Series after so many years as a player and manager; when Dick Vermeil remembered half the plays from the high school championship game he coached, and said that that particular championship was as meaningful to him as his Super Bowl win.

And surprisingly, a few coaches indicated that winning the championship in their respective sport was not the day that gave them the most satisfaction. One instance that really sticks out was when Bill Parcells talked about beating the San Francisco 49ers in the NFC Championship Game in 1990. Parcells won two Super Bowls as a coach, but he didn't mention either. Beating the Niners in San Francisco is what popped into his mind as his best day. I grew up in the 1980s and remember vividly the Giants vs. 49ers as a classic matchup. You had contrasting styles: the Giants' wrecking-ball defense led by maniacal linebacker Lawrence Taylor attacking the Niners' offensive symphony helmed by Joe Montana.

The Niners were the best team for most of the decade, and their coach, Bill Walsh, was considered a genius for his innovative approach. Parcells, on the other hand, was a throwback. His team didn't do ballet, they did smash-mouth football, and in this game, Parcells's construction workers beat the genius's engineers on their home turf, propelling Parcells to his second Super Bowl victory two weeks later. It was here that Parcells began to get credit as a great (not just good) football coach, and he knew it.

As far as my best day, I'll borrow a line from Dan Gable, who won so many championships individually and as a coach, who said he still hopes his best day is yet to come.

What do you consider to be your best day professionally?

RED AUERBACH

"Naturally that would be winning my first championship."

In 1957, in his seventh season as the head coach in Boston, Auerbach's Celtics defeated the St. Louis Hawks in double overtime in Game 7 at the Boston Garden, to clinch their first world championship. Bob Cousy (1957 NBA MVP) and Bill Russell starred for Boston; St. Louis was led by high-scoring forward Bob Petit. The two teams met again in the finals the following year, and St. Louis won in six games.

DUSTY BAKER

"Probably when I needed one home run to reach thirty for the season. I hit it against my nemesis, J. R. Richard. I hit a single my first time up and then a foul-tip strikeout my next time up. And I was the only one left [out of the four best Dodgers players, including Steve Garvey, Ron Cey, and Reggie Smith] who hadn't reached thirty home runs. Four guys had never hit thirty home runs on the same team in the same year. And J. R. Richard was my nemesis and Reggie Smith told him in the first game of the series that I was gonna hit it off of him, and that was the last thing I needed. After I hit that foul tip, I just was muttering to myself, 'I don't think I'm gonna do it.'

"And Tommy Lasorda told me, 'Hey man, you gotta have faith, you know the children of Israel were leaving Egypt and the Lord parted the Red Sea and all this stuff.' I said, 'OK, OK, OK, Tommy, I believe.' And I went back up there and this breaking ball stopped, and I hit it over the center field fence. I'll never forget that one."

On October 2, 1977, Baker hit his thirtieth home run of the season to join teammates Steve Garvey (thirty-three), Ron Cey (thirty), and Reggie Smith (thirty-two) in the thirty-plus home run club. The 1977 Dodgers were the first team in history with four thirty-plus home run players. They would go on to the World Series, eventually losing to the New York Yankees.

BRIAN BILLICK

"Any time you can win a Super Bowl, it's such a rare occurrence; it's a culmination of so many things and a day that you're never, ever going to forget—and not for necessarily the reasons that people would think. Most people, when they think of that day, when they dream of that day, it's probably a selfish dream. It's about yourself: 'Gee, look what I've done, this validates who I am.' But in fact when you're given the grace of that day, it's a very humbling experience because you realize just how many people it took for you to be standing there holding that Lombardi Trophy. It is very humbling but it is a validation of what you do. It now transcends theory to fact. What it takes to win."

On January 28, 2001, the Baltimore Ravens crushed the New York Giants in Super Bowl XXXV, 34–7. The Ravens defense dominated the game, not allowing the Giants to score all day. The only points scored by New York were on a punt return for a TD. Ray Lewis, Baltimore's superstar middle linebacker, was named the game's MVP.

NICK BOLLETTIERI

"Two days: receiving the Arthur Ashe Institute Award at Chelsea Piers in March, and the other that I'll always remember is Andre Agassi winning Wimbledon in 1992. At the dinner that night he looked over to me and said, 'You're responsible for this.' Those two things, how can you ask for anything more than that?"

In 1992, Andre Agassi, who Bollettieri had coached since he was thirteen, won the championship at Wimbledon. It was the first "major" title of Agassi's career. He would go on to win seven more majors in a Hall of Fame career.

BOBBY BOWDEN

Well, the luckiest day, probably, was the day I accepted the Florida State job. I didn't know it then. I came down to Florida State, left West Virginia, where we had just been to a bowl game. Florida State had been 0–11, 1–10, and 3–8. And I left a successful program at West Virginia and came down to Florida State thinking I was only going to stay a few years and leave. This was my part of the country, and actually I was coming home. It ended up one of the best dadgum things that ever happened to me, with what we were able to accomplish here. That was thirty years ago, by the way."

Bowden was named Florida State's head coach in January 1976, and has coached the Seminoles for over thirty seasons. During that time, the 'Noles had a streak of being ranked in the Associated Press's top five for fourteen consecutive seasons—a record unmatched by any team.

SCOTTY BOWMAN

"Best day? It's hard to pick one, but probably the last game I coached, because I didn't know we were going to win the game, but I knew it was my last season coaching and if we won, we'd win the Stanley Cup and I would be retiring as a coach.

"Put everything together and I gotta say that I was always anxious to be a coach that won my last game. Unfortunately when a team is losing and not doing well, the coach gets fired. So usually the coach loses his last game, then gets fired. I was fortunate to be able to win that game and go through with my plan to retire, you know?"

CK:　"Yes, usually it's an involuntary retirement."
SB:　"[Laughs.] Yes."

On June 13, 2002, the Detroit Red Wings captured the Stanley Cup with a 3–1 win over the Carolina Hurricanes in Game 5 of the finals. It was the ninth Cup victory for Bowman and his last game as an NHL coach. He went out on top, as few coaches do.

JOHN CHANEY

"I think, as a coach, when I was selected to become the coach out at Cheyney State. At the time, I had been coaching for six years at Simon Gratz High School. And a great man here in the city wanted me to come out and be the coach there. And I was sort of reluctant about making that kind of a move, because I was comfortable, you know. When you're comfortable, there's a fear factor involved, apprehension about going one way or the other. Especially when you're having the kind of success that I was having at Gratz at the time.

"But I went to Cheyney State and after being there for ten years, we won the national championship in 1978. We were always one of the top Division II teams in the country during the time I was there. Winning that national championship was perhaps one of the greatest things. To see the transformation of so many of our players, working with youngsters who don't normally have the opportunity and access to higher education—that was extremely important to me. It was just so great to see kids so proud of themselves from having accomplished their deed. They looked like men, they dressed like men.

"And they went back, the same team went back in 1979, we went to the finals of Division II that year and couldn't win it, but to see the look on their faces—Cheyney State, who had never won a national championship, to have accomplished that with guys that somebody said 'No' to, guys that came from the ghetto, who couldn't make it in life. Cheyney State gave them a chance and they really proved a lot of people wrong. Every last one of them graduated from school. We developed a great basketball program and a great program in academics as far as tutoring was concerned. Academic support was developed in that university at that time. So I'm pretty proud of that."

CK: "That's a great story. So taking those underprivileged kids and turning them into champions sticks out in your mind?"

JC: "It sticks out even today, and I see every last one of them from time to time, they call me, and, boy, they are doing exceptionally well. It shows you what access, opportunity, and education can do for people. Not the fact that they're given some special privileges, just making education accessible for them, making sure that there is an opportunity for them to advance. You're not gonna say this is the cut-off point for somebody to be educated, which is what I really detest.

"Professor Lawrence Tribe of Harvard University, who is one of the best constitutional attorneys in the country, made it very clear that you cannot test intellectual habits, so no one can predict what someone will do if given access and opportunity and provided with the proper motivation."

As head coach at Cheyney State, Coach Chaney put together a record of 225–59 in ten seasons and was named Division II National Coach of the Year twice. He led his team to the NCAA Division II national championship in 1978.

BILL COWHER

"I'd say certainly seeing a group of men come together and fulfilling the ultimate goal, which would obviously be winning the Super Bowl championship. I haven't experienced that yet and that would be the ultimate. But I think it would be just seeing young men grow and, on any particular day, watching them have success doing something that you've seen them strive hard to do, something they're having trouble with, then you see the persistence and hard work pay off. That's probably the most satisfying part of coaching professionally and coaching period."

After this interview, Cowher got his championship as he led the Pittsburgh Steelers to victory in Super Bowl XL, where they defeated the Seattle Seahawks 21–10. Wide receiver Hines Ward was named the game's MVP.

ANNE DONOVAN

"It's when I can leave practice or a game and feel like I've done my best, and most importantly I've brought out the best in my players. There's a sense of satisfaction that carries me on into the next day and hopefully that translates into a win, but not always."

My interview with Coach Donovan took place before she became the first female head coach to lead her team to a WNBA championship with the Seattle Storm in 2004.

ANGELO DUNDEE

"Best day professionally was the double championships: Louie Rodriguez and Sugar Ramos. *Sports Illustrated* was doing a huge story on Louie then. He finally was gonna get his due, 'cause Louie Rodriguez was a great fighter. And Sugar Ramos was fighting Davey Moore. Ramos-Moore turned out to be a tragedy. This naturally got all the print.

"But I had so many great times; you're gonna say, what about Zaire? And what about the Thrilla in Manila? I got spoiled with Muhammad Ali. What the heck, I mean this is a guy that was the greatest thing that ever happened to boxing and nobody appreciates it better than me. Because we needed him. He was the first guy out of the ring that gave of himself. Every other fighter before that was dese, dems, and dose—my manger does the talking, the trainer, the promoter, whatever. He was the first guy. You know he had to be a very talented guy to get away with that because God forbid if you flubbed, you were in deep trouble. A great man, Muhammad."

A stylish master boxer, Luis Rodriguez captured the welterweight title by unanimous decision in fifteen rounds. He defeated Emile Griffith, who was considered by many to be one of the greatest welterweights of all time. Rodriguez would lose the title back to Griffith six months later on a split decision in Griffith's home turf at Madison Square Garden.

Sugar Ramos battered Davey Moore for the featherweight title. Sadly, Moore died as a result of injuries sustained in that bout. Ramos successfully defended the title three times before losing the crown.

The Thrilla in Manila was fought between Muhammad Ali and Joe Frazier for the world's heavyweight championship on October 1, 1975, at Araneta Coliseum in the capital of the Philippines.

In an epic battle of two great champions, Ali finally prevailed by technical knockout after fourteen rounds, when Eddie Futch, Frazier's trainer, stopped the bout. Both men had given their all and were exhausted physically and mentally. Futch said he stopped the fight because he feared for his fighter's well-being. Ali later described the fight as a near-death experience.

TONY DUNGY

"I've had a lot of good days and a lot of really, really positive things have happened professionally. But I'd have to say being on the winning team in Super Bowl XIII; that's one time where I've been on a team that set a goal and got to the ultimate. When you set that goal and achieved it—it was a great feeling. I played with some tremendous players, and we were able to accomplish that goal that year."

On January 29, 1979, the Pittsburgh Steelers became the first team in history to win three Super Bowls by defeating the Dallas Cowboys in one of the most exciting Super Bowl games ever played, 35–31. Pittsburgh quarterback Terry Bradshaw was named the game's MVP.

HERMAN EDWARDS

"It was probably when I made the Philadelphia Eagles and started the first game of the year as a rookie, being a free agent. Knowing that I had accomplished a lot of things that other people thought I couldn't have done. That was my best day, not to just make the team, but to be a starter."

CK: "It must have felt great."

HE: "[Laughs.] Yeah, but then it was, OK, you've done this, now what? How long can you do it?"

CK: "But when you were standing on that field it must have felt great."

HE: "Oh yeah, when I got introduced on opening day, as the starting corner, as a rookie free agent, that was big for me."

As a player, Herman Edwards signed with the Philadelphia Eagles as an undrafted free agent cornerback in 1977 and played ten seasons in the NFL, making a Super Bowl appearance with the Eagles in 1980.

JEFF FISHER

"From a personal perspective, I believe that we have to have our best day of work after a loss. Most people, anybody and everybody, can handle wins. I think the challenge in professional sports and all sports, even individual sports, is how you respond after losses.

"As a coach, it's our responsibility to put losses in perspective. And going beyond that, probably most important is being able to keep winning and losing in perspective.

"I believe that some of the best days I have had are those days where you just don't know where you're going and you don't want to come to work because the loss is so difficult or devastating. Those are the days where you have to take a deep breath, hold your head up, square your chin up, and go in and pick up those people who are looking to you for answers."

On January 30, 2000, the Tennessee Titans met the heavily favored St. Louis Rams in Super Bowl XXXIV. In the fourth quarter of a close game, with time running out and Tennessee down by a touchdown, the Titans drove to the Rams' ten yard line. Titans quarterback Steve McNair then hit wide receiver Kevin Dyson on a short slant pattern and Dyson sped toward the end zone.

Dyson was going to score, but Rams linebacker Mike Jones tackled him at the one-yard line, just shy of the end zone. Time ran out before Tennessee could run another play. The tackle saved the game for the Rams and handed the Titans a heartbreaking loss. The next season, Fisher was there for his team, guiding them to another 13–3 record in the regular season and a trip to the play-offs.

DAN GABLE

"My best day professionally I hope is yet to come. I always have goals that are above and beyond. Even when you've had accomplishments and done great things, and probably had things that haven't come through, I would hope my most satisfying is yet to come. I'm always looking for higher levels of feelings and accomplishments.

"I don't know what that's going to be. It could be with my family, it could be in my profession, which is wrestling, and I hope it's both. And also, along with those things is faith, and hopefully that will be the high of my life."

After his distinguished wrestling and coaching career, Gable contin-ues to seek new challenges. In addition to being an assistant athletic director at Iowa, he makes frequent appearances supporting and pro-

moting wrestling throughout the United States, and has released several instructional videos. He also wrote a book titled Coaching Wrestling Successfully.

BRAD GILBERT

"One of my ultimates was walking into the Olympic Stadium in Seoul in 1988 with the U.S. team. It was pretty awe-inspiring. That was the first year tennis became a medal sport, and you know, you never thought tennis was gonna become a sport in the Olympics. But getting a chance to walk in, in the Olympics, and then the whole two-week experience where you never hear your name mentioned one time. They don't say 'Game Gilbert,' they say 'Game USA.' I got a bronze medal there, but just walking into the Olympic Stadium was pretty amazing."

CK: "Sounds great. Stadium packed with people . . ."

BG: "Yeah. It goes alphabetically, right? So the United States, we're almost at the very end. It was pretty fun."

Gilbert was the number-five seed in the men's tennis competition at the Seoul Olympics in 1988. His hope of a gold medal ended when he lost to fellow American Tim Mayotte.

Gilbert and Stefan Edberg were awarded bronze medals, Mayotte got the silver, and Miloslav Mecir of Czechoslovakia won the gold.

CARRIE GRAF

"I have a lot of them. The typical or easy answer is to say championship wins or those kinds of things, but for me the best days are when I get a letter from a player that I've coached or a phone call to say 'You really impacted my life.'"

APRIL HEINRICHS

"For me, being a workaholic, with soccer running roughly 360 days out of that year, the best day on the job is unequivocally a game day, when we're playing one of our great rivals. And that feeling you have when you wake up and you're getting prepared for a game.

"I prepare as a coach almost exactly the same as I did as a player. I have a pregame routine and ritual that I go through. And to be facing one of our great rivals in front of a large crowd in a beautiful stadium on a crisp night, with the lights shining, and of course with us having success . . . [laughs] that to me is the best day possible professionally."

Game day for Coach Heinrichs has spanned most of her life. She has been playing and coaching soccer from the time she was a youth, through an illustrious collegiate and professional career, to coaching the U.S. Women's National Team.

WHITEY HERZOG

"Well, I had my best day and my worst day on the same day.

"I was playing for the Washington Senators and I had seven RBIs. We were playing against Cleveland and I had a bases clearing double off of Bob Feller, and a two-run triple against Don Mossy. I looked like I was a hero. We were ahead 8–7, and I had driven in seven runs. Then, on a ground-ball single into center field in the ninth inning, I was the tying run on second base. I should have gone to third where I could've tagged up and scored on the next batter, but I didn't, and we lost 9–8. So I not only had my best day as a player, but went from hero to goat in a matter of minutes.

"Now my best day professionally as a manager would be when we won the World Series. There's nothing like that. That's something that you don't realize what hit you until it happens.

"But I always look at it like tomorrow's gonna be my best day."

The 1982 World Series pitted America's two largest beer-producing cities against each other. St. Louis, home of Anheuser-Busch, met Milwaukee, home of the Miller Brewing Company, in the Fall Classic.

The Cardinals prevailed four games to three, with St. Louis catcher Darrell Porter winning Series MVP.

KEN HITCHCOCK

"I would have to say the day we lost to New Jersey in Game 6 in double overtime. It might have even been triple overtime. That would be my best day because I saw players give everything they had with nothing left to give on both sides. I coached in a hockey game where the level of desperation was beyond anything I'd ever seen or experienced in my life, and I've never seen it at that level since. Ever. By any team, let alone any two teams."

CK: "It's amazing the games that pop into people's minds when I ask this question."

KH: "I mean we've won Cups and championships and gold medals and all that stuff but I've never seen two teams that, from the drop of the puck to the final goal, played with such an unbelievable sense of desperation to a man. I've never seen anything like that in my life."

Eight minutes and twenty seconds into the second overtime, the New Jersey Devils' Jason Arnot ripped a shot past Dallas Stars' goaltender Ed Belfour, ending one of the greatest Stanley Cup games ever, as the New

Jersey Devils prevailed 2–1. It was the second consecutive overtime game for the teams and the victory gave the Devils the 2000 Stanley Cup. Hard-hitting Devils' defenseman Scott Stevens was play-off MVP. The loss ended Dallas's quest for their second straight championship.

BELA KAROLYI

"Because I was always in the coaching profession, it was always the competitions—and having successful competitions and sharing the success with my own athletes. Those were always the most uplifting and unbelievable moments.

"But at the same time, sharing the failure is also something that I appreciate very much. I always appreciated that I could share that with them. Sharing the success and the failure with the one you work with, the one you put your heart into. You share the feelings and the end result of your common work. I appreciated that very, very much through my coaching career."

CK:　"Does any one day come to mind?"

BK:　"Well, many great days, but the one that with the years becomes more and more beautiful, just like a first love, is 1976, Montreal. When the little Nadia became Olympic champion of the world."

CK:　"The perfect 10s."

BK:　"Those falling perfect 10s. The first time ever in the history of the sport. That is something that I would call a dream moment."

In 1976, at the Olympics in Montreal, Karolyi student Nadia Comaneci dazzled the world by recording the first perfect 10 in the history of Olympic gymnastics competition.

At four-feet-eleven, eighty-six pounds, the thirteen-year-old became the darling of the games and would receive seven perfect 10s through-

out the competition. She won five medals: three gold, one silver, and one bronze, and became the world's most famous gymnast.

TRUDI LACEY

"I think my best day is when I teach a player either a skill or a life lesson and then I watch them use that and have success."

MARVIN LEWIS

"Winning the Super Bowl. Being on a team that wins the Super Bowl."

As defensive coordinator of the 2000 Super Bowl champion Baltimore Ravens, Marvin Lewis presided over one of the NFL's best-ever defenses. During the regular season, they allowed only 165 points, the fewest amount since the NFL went to a sixteen-game schedule in 1978. In the play-offs, the defense gave up a mere sixteen points, on one offensive touchdown and three field goals in four games, for an average of four points per play-off game!

LUTE OLSON

"It was probably the day I was notified that I had been elected to the Naismith Hall of Fame. From a coaching standpoint, that's really the top of the list when you're honored with induction into the Hall."

A devoted family man, when Olson was inducted into the basketball hall of fame in 2002, he chose to attend his son's wedding in Italy instead of the induction ceremony, stating, "It's a shame it's the same weekend but family comes first."

TOM OSBORNE

"I suppose, referring to coaching, many might say that winning the Orange Bowl and staying undefeated against Miami in 1995, where we beat them down there 24–17. We came back to win in the fourth quarter, which usually is hard to do when you play Miami in Miami. They usually out-condition you or the humidity and the weather takes a toll. We weren't the strongest team in the fourth quarter and there were the usual complaints about not winning a national championship, so that answered many of those questions.

"But I might also add that there was another game in the Orange Bowl against Miami at the end of the 1983 season. The 1984 Orange Bowl, eleven years before, in which we lost, we went for two points at the end of the game and the ball was tipped away and we lost 31–30. We had been down 17–0 early in the game and came back to have a good chance to win it and I thought that was a great game. It was a well-played game. We didn't happen to win it, but that also was a game that I'll remember.

"There was another game where we missed a field goal right at the end—it was the 1994 Orange Bowl. We played Florida State and they had, in terms of talent, probably one of the most talented teams ever. And we played well enough to win that night. So I didn't really measure great days so much in terms of final outcome but more in terms of how we played and what we did with what we had.

"Those three games certainly stand out in my mind."

Interestingly, in the 1983 Orange Bowl, Nebraska scored a touchdown near the end of regulation to pull within 31–30, and the extra point would have tied the score, assuring Nebraska of at least a share of the national championship. Coach Osborne, however, played for the win, and the two-point conversion failed, giving Miami sole claim to the number-one ranking.

Because of this, critics labeled Osborne as a coach who could not win the big game. He emphatically silenced his doubters in the 1990s, however, by winning three national championships in his final four seasons.

BILL PARCELLS

"Now that's a hard one. I think probably the greatest feeling I had was in 1990 in the play-offs when San Francisco had kind of been the dynasty, and they were going for their third straight Super Bowl. We had lost our quarterback, Phil Simms, and had a backup (who was pretty good, by the way) named Jeff Hostetler.

"We went to San Francisco and won the NFC Championship and then eventually to the Super Bowl and beat Buffalo. That particular game, if I had to name one game, was probably it. It was a 15–13 score. We were such underdogs, and then the drama in the game, it came down to us kicking a field goal with three seconds left."

The 1990 NFC Championship Game was a clash of NFL titans, with the New York Giants visiting Candlestick Park in San Francisco to challenge the two-time defending champion 49ers.

The entire game was a defensive battle, with only one touchdown being scored, on a sixty-one-yard dart from Montana to John Taylor, putting San Francisco up 13–6 early in the third quarter. The Giants could not get in the end zone, but kicked two more field goals to pull within 13–12 in the fourth quarter. After a 49ers fumble late in the fourth quarter, Giants kicker Matt Bahr kicked his fifth field goal of the game (an NFC Championship record) to give the Giants a 15–13 win.

After the game, Coach Parcells said, "That's what championship football is supposed to be about. Hey, they got great players, I think we got some great players, and you guys just saw a hell of a game."

MIKE SCIOSCIA

"It's really tough to narrow it down to one day. I mean, I have a career that I look back on and it was very satisfying, very fulfilling to pursue a dream you have as a youngster, and to play it out is something not a lot of people get to do, and I'm very grateful for that.

"To narrow it down to one game or one day is virtually impossible. I was a part of two world championship teams as a player and one as a manager. I think the day you win or clinch a world championship is really the ultimate if you're in professional baseball."

Mike Scioscia was a backup catcher on the 1981 Dodgers team that defeated the New York Yankees in the World Series four games to two. In 1988, he was the starting catcher as the Dodgers defeated the Oakland A's four games to one to win the title. Then, in 2002, Scioscia won his first championship as a manager, leading the Anaheim Angels to victory over the San Francisco Giants four games to three.

TUBBY SMITH

"The day that I became a high school teacher and coach. And it happened kind of accidentally because I was going into the air force and I went home to southern Maryland, my alma mater, Great Mills High School. I mean I always wanted to teach and coach, don't get me wrong, but the opportunity to go back to my alma mater was the best thing ever.

"That prepared me for everything I go through now because I had the challenge of coaching where I went to school, coaching relatives, with brothers and sisters in the school. Those same folks had helped me become who I am and now I could go and give something back. That was the greatest day of my professional career.

"I would say winning the national championship, but that first day gave me the first opportunity."

Smith began his coaching career at Great Mills High School in Great Mills, Maryland. He was head coach there for four years and compiled a 46–36 record.

The Kentucky Wildcats won the 1998 NCAA men's basketball championship in Tubby Smith's first season as head coach when they defeated Utah 78–69 at the Alamodome in San Antonio, Texas.

EMANUEL STEWARD

"For me as a boxer, nothing will exceed the night that I won the national Golden Gloves title. That was my highlight. Of all these other things, now I've probably had more big moments that any other manager or trainer in history. It's been a long run, you know?

"On that legends night on HBO, we started out with Hearns and finished up with Mike Tyson and Lennox Lewis. And I'm the only guy that's in the first episode and the last episode. A twenty-one-year run, and that's a long time to still be going into Superfights, when pretty much everyone has come and gone in that twenty-one-year span.

"But my best day professionally as a trainer . . . I'll probably say the night that I had Holyfield regain the championship by beating Riddick Bowe. That is one of my greatest, surpassed only by Hilmer Kenty, my first champion, beating Ernesto Espana. That would be my best day professionally—Hilmer Kenty, my first champion. And then the night that Holyfield beat Riddick Bowe, which, you know, he had no chance. The only time he beat Bowe out of the three fights was the one that I trained him for."

On March 2, 1980, Steward's pupil Hilmer Kenty knocked out Ernesto Espana in the ninth round to win the lightweight championship. The fight was held at Joe Louis Arena in Detroit, Michigan, with Joe Louis himself in attendance.

In the second of three memorable fights against Riddick Bowe, Evander Holyfield—under Emanuel Steward's tutelage—won a majority decision to regain the heavyweight title on November 6, 1993.

JOE TORRE

"I have to go to the 1996 World Series, when Charlie Hayes caught a pop-up off Mark Lemke's bat—I think it was October 26, 1996—to win my first World Series.

"Before that, I remember the championship series where we beat Baltimore to go to the World Series and that was very emotional for me. The whole year was emotional, because in the middle of the season my brother Rocco passed away, and I'd be sitting on that bench trying to gain perspective on life, thinking about him. Then later in the season, my brother Frank had to come to New York because he needed a heart transplant. And he happened to get the heart transplant operation the day before we won Game 6.

"So it was a highly emotional year for me, especially to see Frank and talk to him after we won the World Series. He was really proud of me, and here it was—I caught up with him. He had those two World Series rings and I caught up with him and he couldn't be more proud of me."

CK: "I could hear in your voice how important getting that first World Series was to you."

JT: "Yes, and the thing about it is that other people never looked at me as a failure, obviously. I had teammates with the Cardinals who had been in several World Series and there was always something missing for me, because I was always hanging around with these guys and they had all been part of winners. They didn't have to hit .300 or win twenty games, but they were part of a team that won the World Series. And to me, that Cardinal experience was a growing experience because I was surrounded by a bunch of winners when I was playing there."

In 1996, the New York Yankees met the defending champion Atlanta Braves for the World Series. Atlanta won the first two games in Yankee Stadium by a combined score of 16–1, the biggest run differential in World Series history.

The series then headed back to Atlanta for three games, and the Braves appeared to be a cinch to capture their second consecutive world championship. The Yankees stormed back, however, winning four straight games (all three in Atlanta, then Game 6 back in New York) and their first title since 1978. Yankee closer John Wetteland, who saved all four wins, was series MVP.

JOHN TORTORELLA

"I don't want to have one best day, but the best time professionally for me was seeing the group of men that I just coached go through the two-month ordeal and grind of winning a Stanley Cup. I've been involved in this business now for eighteen years as a coach and I know the Stanley Cup is the toughest thing to win. I had the great fortune to go through it with this group of men for two months. That has been the greatest time for me, to see what these athletes had to go through to get the ultimate prize.

"I guess the best time was to sit there after we won the Cup and we kicked all the media out of the locker room, we kicked everybody except the team out of the locker room and spent twenty minutes together to celebrate. I sat in one of the stalls of the players and I watched how they reacted after they accomplished what they did, and that was the most gratifying time for me. To see these athletes celebrate after going through such a grind for two months."

Coach Tortorella continued about the difficulty of getting through the play-offs . . .

JT: "It was cool because you and I can say it's the toughest trophy to win, but myself and my coaching staff were with them every step of the way and watched what they had to do through those two months. Then to see it culminate in your home building and your locker room afterward. That was the neatest thing I've ever been involved in."

CK: "Well, you went through the seven-game series with the Flyers, the seven-game series with Calgary."

JT: "It's amazing. Especially after the Flyers came back and beat us in Game 6. When we almost had that game won in Game 6 and then Primeau scores the goal late, with a minute and a half left and they beat us in overtime. Yeah, I wasn't sure if our team was going to come through and be able to answer in Game 7 after an emotional loss like that—but they did. That was just amazing. To see the mental toughness of the athletes; to go through that and then finally get it done."

DICK VERMEIL

"I'd have to say Super Bowl XXXIV. But I had some other days coming up to that, that were equivalent to it, you know. Like winning the Rose Bowl. Winning the NFC Championship, winning the high school championship; things that are every bit as meaningful in relation to that time in your life."

CK: "On the road to that pinnacle moment . . ."

DV: "Yeah. [Laughs.] I mean I can remember 50 percent of the plays we used in the high school championship game in 1961. So all of those type games that were the ultimate win at that time in my career, remain as part of the ultimate package.

They have the same depth of meaning. And the kids that played on those teams were every bit as great football players in relation to the game they were playing in, as the world champions in Super Bowl XXXIV."

CK: "I imagine that your memories of different teams and different events, even though one is the Super Bowl and one is a high school team, are just as vivid."

DV: "Oh, yes. But most of my memories are based on the kids, the players."

Nineteen years after first appearing in the Super Bowl with the Philadelphia Eagles, Coach Vermeil finally won it all when the St. Louis Rams defeated the Tennessee Titans at the Georgia Dome in Atlanta. Rams quarterback Kurt Warner was named the game's MVP.

BILL WALSH

"That would be when the San Francisco 49ers beat the Dallas Cowboys 45–14 in 1981. I think that was the best day I've had from the standpoint of functioning well and directing my team and having them ready to play. Because the previous year they'd beat us 59–14 and we turned the tables on them in just one short year. We really turned the tables. So that particular day I'll always remember and it could've been the highlight of my career."

CK: "It was 1981, the year of Montana to Clark in the play-offs and you guys beat 'America's Team' and then you sort of became 'America's Team' through the 1980s."

BW: "Yes, soon thereafter."

In 1980, the Cowboys rocked the 49ers 59–14. Some of the 49ers felt the Cowboys had run up the score unnecessarily, and the following season, hungry for revenge, the 49ers crushed the Cowboys 45–14, setting the stage for the classic 1981 NFC Championship game, which San Francisco won.

These two wins fueled San Francisco's reign of football supremacy. In fourteen seasons (1981–94), they won five Super Bowls and appeared in nine NFC title games.

LENNY WILKENS

"A couple of things . . .

"As a player, getting the MVP award in the East-West All-Star Game. Certainly, it proved I could compete at that level with the best of all the players in the NBA.

"And I've been very blessed. I've won a championship with Seattle as a coach. That was huge, because I took a team that everyone said was terrible and turned them around. The first year when I took over they were 5–17, and we turned it around and got to the finals. We didn't win it that year, but we won it the next year.

"And I've been fortunate, I was the head coach of the 1996 Olympic team and we won the gold medal.

"And being named to the fifty greatest players in the history of the NBA.

"And of course, best of all is my family. The most important things to me are my belief in God, my family, and a few friends. And I say a few friends because there are a lot of people who say they're your friends, but you find out the truth sooner or later. [Laughs.]"

As a player, Lenny Wilkens appeared in nine all-star games, winning MVP of the 1971 contest in San Diego. He was the game's leading scorer, with twenty-one points, leading the West to a 108–107 victory.

As a coach, he led the Seattle SuperSonics to the 1979 NBA title, defeating the Washington Bullets four games to one.

Lenny was enshrined in the Basketball Hall of Fame twice, as a player and coach.

JOHN WOODEN

"I don't know if I can pick out any one day as my best day profession-ally. I had many days in the seasons that I had and don't like to say that any one day was better than the others."

CK: "Any thing or group of things come to mind? Is there maybe a cumulative goal that was reached that you would put on top?"

JW: "I worked for fourteen years developing something called the Pyramid of Success. And I'd say it's the acceptance of that that has given me more pride than probably anything else. I have numerous requests for that and I speak on it a lot. I send out over fifteen hundred copies every year and have for many, many years. I give it to other coaches who like to give it to their players. And I provide it to businesses as well. The way that has been accepted and the way other people have appar-ently felt it has been helpful to them [is important to me] because I think there's always great joy in learning that some-thing you've said or done has been meaningful to another. That has given me a lot of personal satisfaction. I'd say next to that was the fact that I think I was able to get across pretty well to all of my players that education is the main thing they're in school for. It's not to play basketball. And I believe the graduation rate of my players would rank right up there with the highest of any school."

CHAPTER NINE

ACHIEVING YOUR DREAMS

This chapter contains one of my favorite answers: "Believe in yourself so much that you counter others' disbelief." When Trudi Lacey said this, I was impressed, since it captured the essence of this project. If a person believes they can do something, they can. History is filled with inspirational stories and examples that prove this to be true. The following are a few that come to mind.

1. The airplane: Think about how the Wright Brothers were ridiculed before they actually got the *Flyer* off the ground at Kitty Hawk. How absurd to think a person could get wood and metal to fly?
2. The telephone: Before it was invented, if you told a person in New York that they would be able to talk to a person in Hong Kong—as if they were in the same room—they would have thought you were insane.
3. The television: How could a person in Alaska see the Super Bowl in Miami better than a person who is actually at the game? Television makes it possible, with countless cameras and microphones recording every play—and most people today cannot imagine life without the television.

Each of these concepts seemed impossible before they were invented. There are many others, and many more to come that we have not even imagined yet. I say "we" because these inventions were made by people like you and me.

And belief in oneself and one's ideas is what made them possible.

If you could give a young person advice on how to achieve their dreams, what would it be?

RED AUERBACH

"There are no shortcuts. You gotta pay your dues, you gotta know your trade, and you've got to pay the price. If you want to go through all that and then do a little more, you've got a good shot."

Coach Auerbach paid his dues. He coached the Washington Capitols of the old Basketball Association of America (which became the NBA in 1950) from 1947 through 1949 before taking over with the Celtics in 1950. He then coached the Celtics for seven seasons before capturing his first world championship.

DUSTY BAKER

"To not be afraid to be different and separate yourself from the pack. And that goes for the time that you're willing to put in. My son now has the same complaints I had as a kid. That the kids he's playing with tire from playing ball and he ends up playing alone a lot. You're gonna have to go a lot of times and be by yourself. Go against what the masses say to do."

Dusty doesn't follow the pack. In an age where most managers make decisions based solely on percentages, Baker has made a name for himself by trusting his gut instinct.

He won't just pinch-hit for a batter or bring in a pitcher solely because the "lefty-righty numbers" indicate a trend. He goes with his baseball intuition, and has often been criticized when his moves don't work out. But more often than not, the results he produces are winners—so much so that he has been named National League Manager of the Year three times.

BRIAN BILLICK

"Have the courage of your convictions. Courage is a relative thing. Courage usually fails not because of any personal inequities, but because there is a lack of conviction. It's easy to throw that word out and to have convictions about one thing or another, but they better be true to you because when you come under attack it's the first thing that's going to wash away. And then you'll lose your courage for sure.

"But have conviction about what you do and have a purpose and a cause and a thought process. Remember, it's not usually something that's earned short term, because those are the convictions that get washed away the quickest. Find something to have a conviction about and the courage will come."

Coach Billick is an outspoken personality with a tremendous amount of confidence in himself.

For example, in only his second season as head coach of the Ravens, Billick said, "I have a lot of confidence in myself. Regardless of what happens in Baltimore, I know I'm a good coach. Nothing can happen here that will shake that belief in myself." He then backed up his words by bringing the Ravens to their first world championship in 2001.

NICK BOLLETTIERI

"Success doesn't come overnight. It is a series of long intervals. It takes a lot of patience, a lot of dedication. Short-term success comes and goes but longtime success means working every single day—and then working harder the next day."

Bollettieri's work days often begin before 7 A.M., where at age seventy-three he is still a hands-on coach, directing student exercises on tennis courts. He often bicycles around the IMG Academy's six-mile training center.

BOBBY BOWDEN

"Number one, when you get a job, treat it like it's the last job you'll ever have. Work like it's the last day you'll have on earth, and do the absolute best that you can. A lot of guys get in a position and start looking way down the road. Where can I get a better job? How can I get promoted? Things like that. Just do the darn best you can, and give it everything you've got and that other stuff will take care of itself."

Coaching the Florida State Seminoles may end up being the last job Coach Bowden ever has. He's taken FSU from a lower level to one of the nation's elite football programs.

SCOTTY BOWMAN

"You have to have some goals ahead of you. You have to have some vision. There are a lot of things you need, but primarily if I could tell a person what you have to have, it is to show patience. Patience is a virtue, it's often said, and it's true."

In 1951, after an injury ended his playing career when he was eighteen years old, Bowman persevered as a coach. Twenty-two years later, his patience was rewarded when he won his first Stanley Cup with the Montreal Canadiens in 1973.

JOHN CHANEY

"Now that's a good one. That is a good one. In today's society there are so many competing forms of negative motivation. There are so many people who bend and twist the truth. And so many people who have somewhat warped ideas about how to motivate youngsters and how to create for them a better life.

"You've gotta understand that with the competition that we have, in trying to talk to youngsters about the right way, the best way, the good way, the good living, that we are competing against negative forces. I remember about three years ago there was a poll taken on the things that influence youngsters—and what things influenced them more than others. There were five things that they listed. The top thing was their peers. The second was TV and entertainment, and the third thing was schools. Tied for fourth and fifth was religion and parents. Now you tell me if something's not wrong here.

"What I'm getting at is when you're trying to talk to a youngster about being successful and how to achieve success, you have to come up with quick, *and I mean quick*, goals for him. There has to be steps for him to undergo to achieve success step-by-step-by-step until he reaches that big goal.

"Kids want instant success. They do not want to work hard enough, long enough to achieve success. So if you're going to get into the head of any youngster today and try to explain to him about success and how to reach success, you better have some steps that will reach a higher level later, but he's gotta experience some success along the way.

"You've got to set goals that they can obtain quickly and then move the marker out. You've gotta keep 'em biting, keep 'em interested, keep 'em motivated until they accomplish something. So when he looks back, he says, 'Did I do that?' Sometimes you've got to trick them. You've got to fool 'em into success."

Since most of Coach Chaney's players didn't go on to become professional athletes, his coaching methods were intended to help youngsters advance to adulthood with discipline, self-esteem, and productive life skills.

BILL COWHER

"Three things I've always said:
1. Never quit anything you start.
2. Work harder than the other person.
3. Never be intimidated by anyone or anything."

Coach Cowher fought his way onto an NFL roster after being cut by the Eagles in 1979. He then worked his way onto two teams as a special teams standout. His Steeler teams are usually the ones intimidating opponents with a hard-hitting defense and bruising running game.

ANNE DONOVAN

"There's no substitute for hard work; it is what sets you up for success. And some of the most successful people in life are the ones who work the hardest. If you look at the players in the WNBA, the ones that work the hardest may not be the most talented or most successful right now, but I guarantee they're gonna be successful down the road. Whether it's as a professional player or as a professional in life, because they've got that foundation, which is a work ethic."

During Coach Donovan's playing days she developed a work ethic to match her formidable stature. Hall of Famer Ann Myers-Drysdale said, "She had to work very hard for what she accomplished. She was not strong. She was not quick. There was criticism of her game."

In the 1970s and early 1980s, the Soviet Union and their seven-foot-two, 280-pound center, Uljana Semjonova, dominated international women's basketball. Semjonova overwhelmed Donovan in early matchups. Then in 1986, as she prepared for the Goodwill Games in Moscow, Donovan worked on her strength and conditioning in order to compete with the big Russian. To prepare mentally, she drew a picture of herself blocking Semjonova's shot.

During the games, Donovan not only blocked Semjonova's shot, she had a stellar tournament, averaging 10.9 points and 9.9 rebounds per game. The United States handed the Soviets their first defeat in nineteen years, and Donovan had shown the mental and physical preparation skills that would make her a great coach when her playing career ended.

ANGELO DUNDEE

"Be realistic about what you want to do. You don't really know where life's gonna take you, but whatever you do, treat it good. Try to be the best at what you do. Very simple, very basic, and don't lose that perspective of being nice."

Life led Angelo Dundee from a small, working-class neighborhood in south Philadelphia to New York City to Miami Beach, where he opened one of the most respected boxing gyms in the country. His skills as a trainer and nice-guy persona took him all over the world training the greatest fighters in boxing's biggest matches.

TONY DUNGY

"You have to be determined to get there no matter which way the crowd is going. You can't depend on the crowd to take you there. Sometimes you have to be a leader rather than a follower to be successful and to get to your goals. It's easy to go when all the momentum is going that way and everybody you know wants to do the same things and they're excited about getting there. But that doesn't always happen—in fact, it rarely happens.

"People go opposite ways, in different directions, branching off. And they're not as interested in getting there as you are. You can't depend on other people. You've got to set your course and follow it and be determined. And if you're willing to do that, chances are you're going to be successful."

In Coach Dungy's hunt for an NFL head coaching job, he waited ten years from his first interview in 1986 with the Philadelphia Eagles (the job went to Buddy Ryan), until 1996, when he was hired in Tampa Bay.

When he interviewed for various jobs around the league, Dungy's calm, low-key demeanor was cited as a negative by NFL general managers. Many thought him to be too mild-mannered to be able to motivate NFL players.

In 1996, however, Buccaneers GM Rich McKay saw those perceived weaknesses as strengths and Dungy was given his first head coaching opportunity. He quickly turned around one of the worst franchises in NFL history. In two short years, the Bucs made the play-offs and won a play-off game. In 1997, Coach Dungy won Coach of the Year honors from several media sources.

HERMAN EDWARDS

"I'd say what my father told me—have your priorities lined up right. Then choose your friends wisely, and don't let them choose you. And if you have the right priorities, you'll choose the right friends."

Two of Coach Edwards's close friends in the NFL are fellow coaches Tony Dungy and Dick Vermeil.

JEFF FISHER

"I would emphasize how important it is to work on your weaknesses every single day. We all have been given strengths, but we have to work on the weaknesses and turn them into strengths in order to realize our potential.

"That player who is a great intermediate receiver and averages six to eight catches a game on the intermediate routes, yet lacks the ability to go downfield—every day he needs to work on his downfield skills because he already has the intermediate skills. You must work on the weaknesses every day. You must do something to affect them.

"In addition, do something on a daily basis to improve your attitude, your skills, and your knowledge. On a daily basis."

DAN GABLE

"In wrestling, the hand gets raised of the winner of the match. But many times, the person whose hand didn't get raised still walks away a winner. And only that person will be able to figure that out. That's because they know what they went through to get there. You don't cut any corners. You leave no stones unturned. You do whatever is needed, from a reasonable point of view, so that when you're done, you can handle the situation as positively as you can."

BRAD GILBERT

"Everybody wants to say you should have success, you know, some of these motivational speakers. But everybody's success level is different. And I think it's most important that you try to be a good person, and try to be conscientious and do the best you can.

"When all these parents ask me, 'What's the most important thing?' For me, it's that you're doing it for yourself. Not for your parents, not for your coach. If you really want to become good, or you want to do things, do it because *you* want to do it. You should be driven by yourself."

Gilbert got the most out of his ability during his playing career. He "won ugly" and worked his way to become one of the top players in tennis during the 1980s. He was ranked in the top ten for nine years, and then rose to number four in the world in 1990.

APRIL HEINRICHS

"I do give a lot of kids some advice, and I go back to what has helped me achieve what I have and to get to where I am: a laser focus with a commitment to outwork anyone. I refuse to be outworked in anything I do.

"Certainly with young people today, there's not a lack of talent, there's not a lack of opportunity, but sometimes you have players that work hard that don't have the talent and vice versa."

Coach Heinrichs brought up a topic she frequently speaks about . . .

"So my advice would be, first and foremost, to decide what you want. I often give a presentation called the Eight Soccer Keys to Life. And the number one thing is to *want something*. Want to be a soccer player, want to be a coach, want to be a newspaper writer or a sportswriter, an author, want to be a biologist or a professor. Once you have that want, that ambition, then set the goals and plan in place. There's a litany of things you go through in terms of that process, but wanting something, identifying that it's achievable and setting goals to achieve it, putting a plan and work ethic in place, reevaluating your goals and then overcoming any obstacles by being willing to overcome them, will more than likely get you where you want to be."

WHITEY HERZOG

"It's very simple: work hard. Try to be the best at anything you do. I don't care what you're doing. If you're in the first grade and you're writing a poem, try to write a good poem. If you're older and you're going to college, work hard, study hard, try to be the best student in the class.

"No matter what you do, always strive to be the best. And that only comes through hard work. You have to work at what you do."

During the 1980s Herzog was widely considered one of baseball's most knowledgeable men and clearly one of its best managers. He earned this respect over a lifetime in the game.

KEN HITCHCOCK

"You should clearly understand that there are many people out there trying to get to the same area you're trying to get to. And understand that there are as many people out there as talented as you are. There are as many people that have as much ability.

"And if you expect to be on top at the end of the day, you're gonna have to put more work in than anybody you're competing against. Don't try to get there just based on your talent. And don't try to get there thinking that somebody owes you something—because it doesn't work that way."

Before becoming a coach, Hitchcock sold hockey equipment at a small sporting goods store in his hometown of Edmonton, in Alberta, Canada. He competed against larger chains that had more merchandise and better prices. He credits this real-life work experience with giving him the confidence to sell himself and his ideas to his players.

BELA KAROLYI

"I would tell them what my mentor told me, 'Be yourself. Follow your own dream. Don't copy anybody, but try to make a healthy, lovely, and enjoyable dream for yourself. One that is going to take you where you want to be.'"

Coach Karolyi helped many young girls achieve the pinnacle of their sport. Gymnast Betty Okino said, "For me, Bela was a mentor and father figure. With his stern glares and bear hugs, he touched the lives of many athletes . . . and made this little girl's dreams come true."

TRUDI LACEY

"Believe in yourself so much that you counter others' disbelief.

"Because we live in a world where many times people look at the negative. Or they look at failure as being final and they want you to hold on to those failures and setbacks. It's the people that can learn from those experiences and continue to persevere toward their goals, no matter how distant the goals seem, no matter how difficult the obstacles, that can achieve their dreams.

"I'll give you an example. When I was in high school I dreamed of being an Olympian, and came very close in 1984, but I didn't play and I thought my dream of becoming an Olympian was over. I went on to do other things—a career in coaching, grad school, playing Europe, and all kinds of stuff—but the dream of being part of the Olympic experience was always embedded in the back of my mind.

"And lo and behold, in 1997, Olympic Basketball called and offered me a job. I was able to work with the men's and women's Olympic team in Sydney and be a part of both of those gold medal teams. From the time I was in high school to the time it happened was twenty years, but I never gave up on that dream. It was something I felt was meant to be a part of my life. I have my own quote, which says, 'If you have the patience to persist, you have the power to prevail.' And that is my mantra. To stay after it, you know? [Laughs.] To show up."

In 1997, Coach Lacey joined USA Basketball as assistant director of women's programs, developing and implementing women's programs in trials, training camps, and international competition. She worked in this position with both the men's and women's gold medal–winning teams at the 2000 Olympic Games in Sydney, Australia.

MARVIN LEWIS

"Have a clear vision. Put together a plan. And don't let anybody set limits on what you can do."

In 2003, Marvin Lewis earned his first head coaching job in the NFL when he took over the perennially losing Cincinnati Bengals. His vision and plan were clear: Build a winner.

The Bengals were the league's most improved team in 2003, and Coach Lewis finished second behind Bill Belichick of New England in the AP voting for NFL Coach of the Year.

LUTE OLSON

"In the selection of their life's goal, if they're going to be successful and going to be happy, they have to do something they're passionate about."

Olson's passion for basketball is well-known. He's an outspoken voice demanding respect for basketball in the west, often citing an "East Coast bias" in the media.

TOM OSBORNE

"First of all, you need to pursue an endeavor that fits your interests and abilities. People always do better if it's something they enjoy doing, something that they have some natural inclination or ability toward.

"Sometimes you see somebody going to medical school because they want to make a lot of money or because their father told them that's what they oughta do. I don't think those people are ever as successful as people who really follow their own interests, their dream, their passion, whatever it may be.

"The other thing I would add would be perseverance. Just the ability to hang in there, to go through the tough times, and of course—as I mentioned earlier—the issue of character becomes very important."

Coach Osborne hung in there for twenty-five years as head coach at Nebraska, not winning a national championship in his first twenty-one seasons. He then caught fire, winning three in his final four years (1994, 1995, and 1997)—the Cornhuskers were 60–3 during that span.

BILL PARCELLS

"Persist. Stay with it. Don't expect instant gratification. Stay with it and be determined."

In his first year as head coach of the Giants, the team went backward from a 4–5 record in the strike-shortened 1982 season, to a 3–12–1 record in 1983. Parcells was almost fired, but he kept his job and stuck with his philosophy of a ball control offense and aggressive defense. The Giants rebounded in 1984, making the play-offs as a wild-card team, and two years later, they won their first Super Bowl.

MIKE SCIOSCIA

"I could only speak for myself and what helped me achieve my goals. You always have that goal in mind but you have to focus on the day-to-day and inch-by-inch steps to reach that goal, and not the huge mountain that's confronting you. Don't focus on the obstacles that may be in front of you in order to attain that goal.

"As far as my focus as a player, yeah, I always wanted to make the major leagues, but I remember in the minor leagues understanding what was going to be needed to climb that mountain step-by-step, the day-to-day work you were going to need to put in to reach that goal.

"I think sometimes people lose focus or get blurred by the size of the mountain that the goal is sitting on and they don't see how they can do it. Or they know it's attainable but they don't take the inch-by-inch approach to attain it, and all of a sudden their foundation isn't what it should be and it crumbles.

"So I would say to reach a goal, don't focus on the goal—focus on the path to get to that goal."

This focus on the day-to-day tasks serves Scioscia well during the rigors of baseball's 162-game regular season. His Angels are fundamentally sound, and do all of the little things right, such as bunting, advancing runners, and playing defense.

TUBBY SMITH

"Learn all you can. Get an education.

"Another thing I think is if you have good manners and respect other people, it'll take you so far in life. You probably don't even have to be that educated, just have that quality and those characteristics where you respect others. 'Yes sir, no sir, yes ma'am, please, thank you, can I help you?' Good manners. Respect other people."

Coach Smith graduated from High Point College in North Carolina in 1973, where he was an all-conference player as a senior. He earned a bachelor of science degree in health and physical education.

He's known to have a southerner's gentle accent and polite manners, often greeting each person at the scorer's table before Kentucky's games.

EMANUEL STEWARD

"Well, the basic bottom line is that as a rule, but not always, you usually get out of something what you put into it. It doesn't happen all the time but most of the time it does.

"Next, try to get things that are realistic, things that are compatible with you and your makeup. I mean is being a basketball player realistic when you're only five-foot-two? Or you want to be a super salesman but you don't really like being around people. Find something that's compatible and realistic with your personality. Set your goals high. The higher you set your goals, the more you're going to have to be willing to sacrifice. Bigger goals require the element of risk.

"And then you're just going to have to work your ass off. And stay focused. Most people undersell themselves on their accomplishments and a lot of it is because they don't have the dedication to be disciplined enough. Discipline is very important. Preparation is the key to so many things."

In 1972, when Emanuel Steward was trying to get Kronk Gym off the ground, he worked for Detroit Edison during the day, trained fighters in the evenings, and did extra electrical work on the weekends to make ends meet. At one point, he had to sell his watch to pay for gasoline during a road trip when he was taking his boxers to a tournament. He risked everything he had for his fighters and the career he believed in.

JOE TORRE

"Work at it. Nothing comes easy. I know that sometimes when you realize how much money people make and how little they seem to work, you have to understand that there's a lot that goes on behind the scenes that you don't know about.

"My mom taught me a lesson: There's a reason for everything happening. And that keeps me from living in the past. It keeps me from being sorry that I put on a hit and run, or changed the pitcher, because you have to deal with reality and deal with the present. And probably that's the best advice I can give. Move on, you can't live in the past, you've got to live right now. Because if you're still thinking about what happened yesterday, you're really cheating yourself."

JOHN TORTORELLA

"It's believing in yourself, believing in how you're doing it. And really, it's a constant evaluation of yourself mentally. As a coach, as a player, as a businessperson, as a young person just trying to find his way, I think you need to go through constant self-evaluation, and sometimes maybe readjusting your mental approach and how you're trying to do things.

"It comes back to adversity: the ups and downs that everybody has to go through in life, and being able to handle that mentally. That is mental toughness and I guess the advice is, if you think it's right, follow through. Just don't give in. Three words that we use a lot: Don't give in. Once you start giving in and you think it may be too tough, that's when it gets you. That's when you begin your slide down the wrong road.

"Don't allow yourself to give in. If you have a true belief, and you want to be successful, there are going to be ups and downs through that road. The key is you just can't give in."

Coach Tortorella was emphatic about the mental toughness a person needs to succeed. He brought it up a couple of times, and delivered his message with an almost confrontational—but still friendly—urgency.

DICK VERMEIL

"Keep defining what it is you want to be, then raise the standard each time you reach it. It's more a destination than a specific goal. My goal was to be a coach in high school. Well, I was a high school coach in my second year in coaching. I just kept coaching and every time a better job was offered to me, I took it.

"So I think you define what it is you want to be and just keep striving to do it better. And it will usually result in you doing something way beyond what you originally set out to do. But just don't stop."

Coach Vermeil has raised the standards wherever he has gone. In high school, he coached the football and swimming teams to championships. At the collegiate level, he brought the UCLA football program back into national prominence. In the pros, he turned around the Philadelphia Eagles franchise, bringing them to the Super Bowl in 1980, and then in 2000 he won it all with the St. Louis Rams.

BILL WALSH

"Look at the short term of improving. Watch other people; learn from other people. Listen to whoever's coaching you. Try to improve every day that you practice and every game that you play. That is the key."

Coach Walsh learned from some of football's greatest minds, including his college coach and mentor Bob Bronzan, and NFL legends Paul Brown, Sid Gillman, and Marv Levy.

LENNY WILKENS

"I'd tell them to really think about what it is you want to accomplish and why. And if it still makes a lot of sense to you, then it takes a lot of hard work. You can't be distracted by what someone says, you've got to work at it every day. It's not going to be easy.

"One of the things I try to ask young people is, 'What's your goal?' If they tell me they want to be a doctor, then I ask them if they know all of the things that surround being a doctor, the things associated with being a doctor. Because sometimes we pigeonhole ourselves and if we widen the spectrum, the chances for success become greater.

"It's like a kid who wants to be a professional athlete, I talk to them about the people who play sports, and that the percentage who make it to the professional level is very small. But if you think about all the people associated with sports—doctors, lawyers, advertisers, promoters, you can see that the spectrum is wider. Maybe you don't get to be the player, you get to be the owner. [Laughs.] So I don't want them to pigeonhole themselves. I tell them to have a broader perspective."

As a kid, Wilkens's basketball career almost never began. He was the last man on his high school team as a freshman and didn't go out for the team in his sophomore and junior years because he thought he wasn't good enough.

After playing in neighborhood Catholic Youth Organization leagues for a couple of years, he was encouraged by a close friend to try out for the high school team. He played as a senior, but graduated midyear and needed a recommendation from his mentor Father Mannion in order to receive a scholarship to Providence College.

Once at Providence, Wilkens quickly established himself, leading the freshman team to a 23–0 record in 1956–57. In his three varsity seasons Wilkens averaged 14.9 points, and he became known as a defensive standout. As a senior, he was named MVP of the NIT Tournament and made two first team All-American teams.

The St. Louis Hawks selected Wilkens in the first round of the 1960 NBA draft.

JOHN WOODEN

"Set a realistic goal, one not so idealistic that it's unattainable and then follow the cornerstones of the Pyramid: working hard and showing your work."

In 1934 Coach Wooden put in place the first two blocks of his Pyramid of Success. They are the cornerstones of the system, and he considers them most essential to success: industriousness and enthusiasm. He defines them as follows:

"Industriousness: I mean very simply that you have to work and work hard. There is no substitute for work. Worthwhile things come only from work.

"Enthusiasm: By that I mean simply that you have to like what you're doing; your heart must be in it. Without enthusiasm you can't work up to your fullest ability."

CHAPTER TEN

FAVORITE QUOTES OR SAYINGS

Y ou waste time and time will waste you."
This is a mantra my father used to say over and over to my brothers and me when we were kids. I don't know if he heard it somewhere or made it up himself, but it was one of his favorite lines and it still haunts me. I know he was trying to get inside our heads and motivate us. He wanted us to get involved in things and apply ourselves, because if we wasted our time, we'd waste our abilities.

Scary stuff for a little kid, but my father's psychology usually worked as a motivator for me. This simple statement still whispers in my ear, and pushes me to work hard even today.

This was a fun question for the coaches, and some of them had answers immediately. Red Auerbach's deadpan delivery of "Show me a good loser and I'll show you a loser" is one of my favorites. And Scotty Bowman actually called me back the next day with two more quotes. This surprised me because I had known of Bowman's reputation as a hard-nosed coach. During our interview, however, he was very cordial, and the fact that he thought about the question overnight and called me back to add two more quotes certainly impressed me.

One of the more revealing and thought-provoking quotes came from John Chaney, but it wasn't really a quote, it's more of a philosophy. He said he wished people could revisit themselves as children to see if they were treated the right way. If they weren't and could go back and change it, would they?

I was lucky to have been surrounded by good people and treated the right way as a kid, but not everyone is. We can't go back and change how we were treated, but we can definitely control how we treat people today and in the future.

What is your favorite quote or saying?

RED AUERBACH

"Show me a good loser and I'll show you a loser."

This quote, delivered in his gravelly voice, captures Coach Auerbach's attitude: He hates losing and loves winning.

DUSTY BAKER

"A man who walks and believes in God will always reach his destination."

Baker, a Baptist, believes there's a heaven and a hell, saying, "I believe that if there's a north, there's a south; that if there's heaven, there's hell; that if there's God, there's a devil. I believe that I've been full of both of them at some point in time."

BRIAN BILLICK

"Wow, it's hard to pull out one, but one that does come to mind is Colin Powell's 'Don't let your ego be so closely tied to your position that when your position comes down so does your ego.'"

Colin Powell was the sixty-fifth secretary of state, serving under President George W. Bush.

NICK BOLLETTIERI

"I've changed my whole philosophy in my motivational speeches. I used to say to everybody, 'Be the best that you can be.' Now I say, 'That's a cop-out. You go out and bring me home the bacon and don't come home until you bring home the bacon.' That attitude gives a person the feeling that I believe in them, that they're gonna believe in themselves. They may not bring home the bacon, but I'm not giving them an option. I want the bacon to come home."

Nick Bollettieri appears regularly as a motivational speaker, has written five books, and has made eleven instructional videos.

BOBBY BOWDEN

"Something like this: 'You can only do your best.' Let's put that ahead of winning. Just do the best you can do, that's all you can do. I hammer that a lot to my players."

SCOTTY BOWMAN

"I have a few. One that was told to me a long time ago is, 'If you do your best, the worst won't happen.'"

Coach Bowman actually thought about this question overnight, and left me a voice mail the next day asking me to call him back. When I did, he offered me two more quotes: "Another one I heard is, 'I can take a lot of aggravation from a .300 hitter and none from a .200 hitter.'

[Laughs.] And another one of my favorites is, 'There's nothing so uncertain as a sure thing.'"

JOHN CHANEY

"I just wish that people would have an opportunity to revisit themselves as children. Revisit how they were raised and how they were treated and take a look at and see if they were treated the right way. If the right thing happened for them to be the kind of human being that they are now. And if they look back, would they want to revisit it and change into being somebody that's better?"

Coach Chaney's philosophical answer reflects his experience with inner-city kids, and his own upbringing.

BILL COWHER

"Right now, where I'm at, my favorite quote is kind of a way of keeping things in perspective: 'You're never as good as you think you are, and you're never as bad as they say you are.'"

Cowher's Steelers have consistently been very good, posting winning records in eleven of his fourteen seasons as head coach.

ANNE DONOVAN

"Do the right thing."

ANGELO DUNDEE

"Be nice, it don't cost nothing."

Angelo's entire message was about how important it is to be a nice person; he mentioned it several times.

TONY DUNGY

"My favorite is probably one that I kinda stole from Denny Green, who I worked with: 'Expectation and execution. No excuses, no explanations.'

"That's something I talk about with my teams every year. That's what we're all about—expectation is what you think, execution is what you do. Excuses and explanations are what you say. We're more interested in thoughts and productivity and not so interested in talk."

Coach Dungy served under then Minnesota head coach Denny Green as the Vikings' defensive coordinator from 1992 to 1995. He often credits Green and former Steelers head coach Chuck Knoll as his mentors.

HERMAN EDWARDS

"Probably 'Where your treasure is, there your heart will be also.'"

CK: "Who said that?"
HE: "That's one of my deals. [Laughs.] I come up with these things.
        "And a great one my dad told me when I was growing up that always stuck with me—this is probably the best one of all, and I told it to my son: 'Son, in life I can't give you a lot of money. I can't give you that, but I'm going to give you

something better than money that you're gonna have the rest of your life. I'm gonna give you a good name.' And when I got older I understood what he said, and he's right. He gave me a good name, and I can't screw it up."

Coach Edwards's father would be extremely proud of his son. He has carried on his father's name with honor. His reputation in the NFL is of a man of character and principle.

JEFF FISHER

"Two days after our Super Bowl loss, we had a parade in Nashville. And as the parade was winding down and the cars were arriving down at the stadium, I looked off to my right and there was a woman holding a sign that said, 'A setback is a setup for a comeback.'

"That captured my attention and provoked a great deal of thought, to the point where I mentioned it publicly to a writer, and it put in print that I was moved by this sign that the woman was holding. A week later I received a copy of a book by Tim Storey, called *It's Time for Your Comeback.* And in the book he talks about that; anytime you have a setback, your comeback has already begun. And everybody loves a comeback story. After our Super Bowl loss, our players were already excited about coming back.

"On September 11, our nation faced one of the biggest setbacks in modern-day history. Yet, moments after that tragic event, our comeback was taking place. It was already taking place. So I believe that 'a setback is a setup for a comeback' is the truth."

DAN GABLE

"Right now there's one out there that I like that says, 'Once you've wrestled, everything else in life is easy.'"

BRAD GILBERT

"My coach used to tell me when I was young, when I turned pro, that negativity breeds. If you're around negative people they'll bring you down. He said to try to surround yourself with positive people, people that have a good attitude, because having a good attitude is infectious and it's contagious.

"You know, I don't think of myself as a guru. I don't think of myself as anything. I just try to live day to day, and I've been fortunate. I think being humble is more important than anything else in this business."

Brad Gilbert is one of the best coaches in tennis, and positivity breeds in his program. He focuses on his players' strengths and develops personal relationships with them outside of tennis.

CARRIE GRAF

"I think the quote that I most like about success is Ralph Waldo Emerson's about a garden patch and a healthy child."

To laugh often and much,
to win the respect of intelligent people and the affection of children,
to earn the appreciation of honest critics and endure the betrayal of
*   false friends,*
to appreciate beauty,
to find the best in others,
to leave the world a bit better, whether by a healthy child, a garden
*   patch, or a redeemed social condition;*
to know even one life has breathed easier because you have lived.
This is to have succeeded.

Ralph Waldo Emerson (1803–1882) was an American thinker and writer famous for his Unitarian views.
Coach Graf recited a portion of the quote by heart.

APRIL HEINRICHS

"Like anyone, I probably go through phases, but I'll say, 'Even if you're on the right track, if you just sit there you'll get run over,' by Will Rogers."

Will Rogers (1879-1935) was an American humorist and entertainer known for his sharp wit and political commentary.

WHITEY HERZOG

"A lot of times I'd say to my ballplayers when I was managing and we'd play a bad game—I'd never close the clubhouse to the press after a game or have a cooling-off period—but I'd walk in the clubhouse and I'd say, 'You guys played tonight like you're trying to get me fired, for crying out loud.' [Laughs.] That'd kind of loosen 'em up a little bit."

Throughout his career, Herzog was one of the game's more colorful, quotable managers.

KEN HITCHCOCK

"If it was easy, everybody would be a champion."

Coach Hitchcock is one of only six active NHL coaches to have won a Stanley Cup.

BELA KAROLYI

"Sometimes I tell the kids, 'The mountains are high, but you are more powerful than the mountains.' It's very suggestive and that's the saying I've used many, many times. Climbing the Himalayas proves the ultimate human potential. The mountains are high, but they've all been climbed by human beings and you are a human being. You can succeed!"

Coach Karolyi's enthusiasm came across as he told me this. His booming voice gets your attention and his encouraging words are like the bear hugs he often gives his athletes.

TRUDI LACEY

"One of them is 'Impossible is an opinion and what's yours?'

"Because many things that people can achieve or have achieved, [other] people initially said was impossible, like Thomas Edison with the lightbulb. It really comes down to what *you* think and what *you* believe. How *you* measure what's impossible to *you*. And I think if you can look at all the possibilities and not look at what's impossible or improbable, then you'll be far more successful."

Coach Lacey's thought-provoking and positive messages are the things I most remember about our interview.

MARVIN LEWIS

"They don't care what you know until they know that you care."

Lewis's passion has won over his players and they are winning games in bunches. In 2005, the team made their first play-off appearance in fifteen years.

LUTE OLSON

"The quote by Theodore Roosevelt about the critic:

"'It is not the critic who counts, not the man who points out how the strong man stumbled, or where the doer of deeds could have done them better. The credit belongs to the man who is actually in the arena; whose face is marred by dust and sweat and blood; who strives valiantly; who errs and comes short again and again; who knows the great enthusiasms, the great devotions, and spends himself in a worthy cause; who, at the best, knows in the end the triumph of high achievement; and who, at worst, if he fails, at least fails while daring greatly, so that his place shall never be with those cold and timid souls who know neither victory nor defeat.'

"The other one would be:

"'What you are shouts so loudly that I cannot hear what you are saying.'"

The quote by Teddy Roosevelt is one of my personal favorites. Roosevelt was the twenty-ninth president and was known for his "macho" image. He boxed voraciously and was an avid outdoorsman. He won the Nobel Peace Prize in 1906 for his mediation in the Russo-Japanese War.

TOM OSBORNE

"A verse of scripture that impacted me quite strongly was something I mentioned to our players before we went out and played Florida for the national championship in the Fiesta Bowl in 1996, which was right after the 1995 season. It's in 2 Timothy 1:7, and it just says, 'For God has not given us the spirit of timidity, but of power and love and self-discipline.'

"And the reason I mentioned that to them was that I don't think you can accomplish anything and be timid. You have to be willing to stick your neck out. And they were certainly not a timid group.

"And also I think the most powerful emotion is love. You can motivate more effectively if people care about each other than if you preach hatred, particularly in athletics. We never talked about hating our opponents, but rather respecting them. And above all, having great cohesion within our team; we felt the more our players cared about each other and the coaching staff, the more cohesive we were and the better we were.

"That particular team that year had gone through a lot of adversity and had become very close. They did have a lot of love, and cared about each other. They also had a lot of self-discipline. Of course discipline is what gets you from point A to point B. They had to work very hard.

"So that particular verse of scripture had a lot of meaning to me, particularly on that occasion, and it has stayed with me since that time as well."

Upon retiring from Nebraska, Osborne, a devout Christian, wrote Faith in the Game, *a book detailing his career at Nebraska and how he implemented Christianity into his coaching techniques.*

BILL PARCELLS

"Something along these lines: 'Talent is a common thing. It's wasted, it's abused, it's disregarded. It's what you do with your gift, whatever that is, that matters.'

"I think a lot of us have gifts in certain areas, but what are you doing about it? How are you manifesting it? Where are you going with it? There may be a lot of guys like you sitting around out there but they don't have the wherewithal to get out and compete. They don't want to be scrutinized. They don't want their work to be evaluated."

Parcells's desire to compete has brought him out of retirement twice, to take on new challenges with different franchises in the NFL. He is one of the most traveled and most successful coaches in league history.

MIKE SCIOSCIA

"My favorite saying is very clear, and it came from my mom. She said, 'You can tell a lot more about people when things are going bad than you can when things are going good for them.'

"That rings true, you know, when you're relating with people and you're meeting people, the best way to judge them is when things go poorly.

"You're gonna get a lot more insight into what makes them go. I've found that to be so true. Some of my closest friends are people that through adversity have gone the extra mile to help people or do things they know they had to do, even though it would've been very easy for them to kind of circle the wagons and lick their wounds.

"You learn more about people when things are going poorly than when things go well."

TUBBY SMITH

"'To whom much is given, much is expected.'

"To me, everything you have has been given to you, it really has. And you need to understand and think along the terms that you have a responsibility and an obligation to repay, to give back."

Coach Smith gives back to the community through various charities, including an annual golf tournament and Tubby's Clubhouses, where he teams with Dell Computers to provide computers and training to underprivileged kids.

EMANUEL STEWARD

"I guess one of the things I always used to write as a motto on a lot of my stationary is: 'A satisfied mind makes no progress.'

"Once you're satisfied, progress stops. If you're satisfied being a contender, you're making about $30,000 to $40,000 per fight, you quit progressing."

We continued talking and Emanuel offered this interesting perspective on his philosophy . . .

CK: "Anything you'd like to add in parting?"
ES: "Life is mental, it's all mental. *You* determine your own fate, your own limitations and failures. *You* determine your own destiny in most cases."

Steward is still active, running Kronk Gym, training fighters, commentating on HBO Sports, and traveling the world for business and speaking engagements.

JOE TORRE

"This is the thing I live by in this game of baseball or even life, and I'm not sure if I heard it somewhere or thought of it myself: 'This is a game where you have to prove yourself to yourself every day.'

"And I think if we live our life that way it keeps us motivated and keeps us from thinking we can't do something, because everybody is capable of doing the best they can. And if you continue to dangle the carrot for yourself it keeps the bubbles going inside. Like when we won the World Series in 1996, my wife suggested, 'Well, that's it, you've filled the gap, let's go.' I said, 'No, I still feel the energy to do this and it's still necessary for me to do it again.' And as long as I have that hunger for it, I'm going to stay as long as someone allows me to and keep trying to do it again."

JOHN TORTORELLA

"The two that stick with me, because they've really been the model of our team this year, are:

"'Safe is death.' Being safe—as far as within our game—is death. I think it speaks for itself. If you're gonna be tentative, and just kind of counterpunch and just touch the water and not go in, then you're gone. You will not succeed. You need to go for it.

"The book that we gave to our team at the beginning of our camp this year, the first line of this book was: 'Good is the enemy of great.' We can be a good team and a lot of guys can be good players and play a long time here. But if you want to be great, you can't allow that to defeat you. And that was our whole process this year. It's a great book, but I don't have it in front of me, it's in my office. I think the title is *Good vs. Great*. It's a great book about a bunch of Fortune 500 businesses that were good businesses, but their CEOs wanted them to be great.

"The three lines that we have in our locker room this year are 'Safe Is Death,' 'Good Is the Enemy of Great,' and 'Don't Think—Do.'"

Published in 2001, Good to Great *is the best-selling book by Jim Collins that studies how fifteen companies went from good to great.*

DICK VERMEIL

"'The main thing is the main thing.'

"I have a good Italian friend of mine named John Scarpa, an entrepreneurial guy who's a very successful businessman and when he uses that term it's from the business world. The main thing there is the money you're making.

"For me it's the quality of your coaching and the goal is the Super Bowl. To win the world championship—that's the main thing. We try to only pay a great deal of attention to the things that make a difference in the main thing. So we don't dilute our efforts with things that don't make a contribution toward getting to the main thing.

"Some people don't know what the main thing is.

"This year we went 13–3 and to me that means we were really good. But in this league good is where you only want to spend a little bit of time as you move toward greatness."

In 2003, the Chiefs finished the regular season with a stellar record, winning the AFC's Western Division. They failed to win the "main thing," though, losing to Indianapolis in the play-offs. Kansas City was the third different team Vermeil has taken to the play-offs (the Eagles and Rams are the others).

LENNY WILKENS

"It is something that was told to me a long time ago and I'll see if I can remember it in order. I was told that if you want to succeed you have to be like a solitary bird, and the conditions for a solitary bird are five:

1. Point your beak skyward. In other words, look forward to things, look up.
2. Fly to the highest point.
3. It will not suffer for company, even of its own kind.
4. Sing very softly.
5. It has no definite color."

In spite of the racism he encountered at various levels, Coach Wilkens has flown to the heights of his profession as a player and coach.

JOHN WOODEN

"My players would tell you what they heard more from me than anything else was 'Be quick, but don't hurry.' I think if you hurry and are out of control you tend to make mistakes. But if you're not quick, you might not be able to get things done. And another one is 'Failure to prepare is preparing to fail.' I think my players would relate to that."

Fittingly, Coach Wooden ended our interview with words that encapsulate the overall feeling I got from the group of coaches.

CK: "Is there anything else you'd like to add that would help people attain the success they set out to reach?"

JW: "Don't give up. Keep plugging. Know that the road to anything worthwhile is not going to be easy and it shouldn't be. There'll be obstacles along the way. You may have to change your method. You may have to back up, you may have to go around, you may have to go over, under. But don't give up. Know that good things are difficult to achieve and that's exactly the way it should be.

"I like a statement that was once said that goes, 'When I look back it seems to me, all the grief that had to be, left me when the pain was over stronger than I was before.' I try to get that across, that difficulties only make you stronger if you accept it that way."

CHAPTER ELEVEN

COACHES' BIOGRAPHIES

Success isn't accidental. It takes a combination of things, including knowledge, a strong work ethic, a good attitude, action, perseverance, and some luck. The coaches should know. Cumulatively, they have helped their teams and students win the following titles:

Forty-five boxing world championships

Twenty-two tennis Grand Slam championships

Seventeen NBA world championships

Sixteen Olympic gold medals

Fifteen gymnastics world championships

Fifteen NCAA wrestling championships

Twelve NCAA men's basketball championships

Eleven Stanley Cup championships

Eight Super Bowl championships

Six World Series championships

Five NCAA football championships

Two Australian WNBL championships

One WNBA world championship

ARNOLD "RED" AUERBACH— PRIDE OF THE CELTICS

Birth date: September 20, 1917

Birthplace: Brooklyn, New York

Claim to fame: Legendary Celtic coach and president

Appropriate quote about Auerbach: "When I came to the Celtics there
was this Celtic mystique. And I was one of the few skeptics. Finally,
it came through to me after we had won the championship. I went
up to Red and said, 'Now I understand what the Celtic mystique is.'
And he was about the proudest man in the world."
                                    —*Paul Silas, former Celtics player and former NBA head coach*

Red Auerbach is generally considered to be the greatest coach in the
history of the NBA. His Boston Celtics have won sixteen world
championships, including nine in his last ten seasons as head coach,
and another seven after he moved to the front office.

Born to a Russian immigrant father and American mother, Auerbach's work ethic and style as a coach reflected the hard-nosed values and dogged determination that would be expected from a
Depression-era child. The Auerbach-coached Celtics did not always
have the most talented players, but they played and won as a team.

In 1956, Auerbach made one of the best deals in NBA history
when he obtained a lanky, active center named Bill Russell, who had
led the University of San Francisco to two NCAA championships. In
Russell, Auerbach acquired an on-court alter ego, a player with the
athletic ability and mind-set to execute his philosophy. Russell, with
his defense, rebounding instincts, and outlet passing, was the plat-
form on which the Celtics' dynasty was built. His dedication to winning reflected Auerbach's prime coaching philosophy: The only
number that matters is the final score. Although Russell was often sta-
tistically overshadowed by the larger, more famous center of that era,
Wilt Chamberlain, Russell's eleven career titles tower above Chamberlain's two. The coach-player tandem of Auerbach and Russell is
still considered to be the most successful and best example of a winning combination in the modern history of team sports.

The Celtics of the late 1950s and 1960s dominated the league
with players like Russell, Bob Cousy, John Havlicek, and Sam Jones.
The tradition continued in the 1970s with Jo Jo White and Dave

Cowens, and the 1980s produced Larry Bird, Kevin McHale, and Robert Parish.

In 1968, Red Auerbach was elected to the Basketball Hall of Fame. Thirteen years later, he was named NBA Executive of the Year. He is a member of the Jewish Sports Hall of Fame. Today, Mr. Auerbach lives in Washington, D.C., and still makes frequent trips to Boston to fulfill his duties with the Celtics.

DUSTY BAKER—PLAYERS' MANAGER

Birth date: June 15, 1949
Birthplace: Riverside, California
Claim to fame: Three-time NL Manager of the Year
Appropriate quote about Baker: "It's pretty obvious that he's one of the best in the business. Every player he gets, he gets the most out of him."

—Jim Hendry, Chicago Cubs general manager

Johnnie B. "Dusty" Baker was always a talented athlete. He graduated from Del Campo High School in Carmichael, California, in 1967 as a star in four sports: baseball, basketball, football, and track. Although he wasn't drafted until the twenty-sixth round by the Atlanta Braves in 1967, Hank Aaron said, "Dusty Baker has more potential than any outfielder I've seen in all my seasons with the Braves."

In 1972, Baker began to realize his promise during his first full season in the majors when he batted .321. After being traded to the Dodgers in 1976, Baker became a clutch hitter who performed best when the stakes were high. In the 1977 National League Championship Series, he hit .357 with eight RBIs, including the series-winning home run off future Hall of Fame pitcher Steve Carlton, and was named NLCS MVP. In the 1978 NLCS, he tied a record by hitting .467.

In 1981, Baker was a leader on the Dodgers world championship team, hitting .320 and winning a Gold Glove. He finished his nineteen-year career with a .278 average, 242 home runs, and 1,013 RBIs. He was selected to the NL All-Star team in 1981 and 1982. He retired as a player in 1986.

In 1988, Baker joined the San Francisco Giants coaching staff under manager Roger Craig. He served as the team's first base coach in 1988, then as hitting instructor from 1989 to 1992. In December 1992, Baker was named to replace Craig as manager of the Giants.

With his dark sunglasses and an ever-present toothpick dangling from his lips, Baker quickly became one of the best and most identifiable managers in the game. In a six-year span with San Francisco (1997 to 2002), the Giants finished either first or second in the division, and Baker won Manager of the Year Award three times (1993, 1997, and 2000), becoming the only National League manager ever to do so (former American League manager Tony LaRussa has also won the award three times).

In 2003, Baker moved to Chicago to manage the long-suffering Cubs. In his first season, he guided the Cubs to within five outs of reaching the World Series. He continues to manage the Cubs, and is known throughout the league as a players' manager who gets the most out of his teams because they enjoy playing for him.

BRIAN BILLICK—COURAGE OF HIS CONVICTIONS

Birth date: February 28, 1954
Birthplace: Fairborn, Ohio
Claim to fame: Coached Baltimore Ravens to Super Bowl victory in 2000
Appropriate quote about Billick: "Coach Billick is someone with a proven track record of motivating people to succeed."
   —*University of Maryland president David J. Ramsay*

Billick entered college at the U.S. Air Force Academy and played linebacker as a freshman before transferring to BYU as a tight end in 1976. He was drafted and released by the San Francisco 49ers in 1977, and then had a brief stint with the Dallas Cowboys.

He entered coaching at Redlands in 1977, then coached at BYU (1978), San Diego State (1981–85), Utah State (1986–88), and Stanford (1989–91). While at Stanford, Billick worked under former 49ers head coach Bill Walsh.

In 1992, he jumped to the NFL when he was hired by Dennis Green as the Vikings' tight ends coach. He was promoted to offensive coordinator three games into the 1993 season, and began to make a name for himself as one of the game's brightest offensive minds. In 1998, the Minnesota offense erupted, setting an NFL record for points in a season (556), bolstering his reputation.

In 1999, Billick landed his first NFL head coaching job with the Baltimore Ravens, and made the most of it. In his first season he led the Ravens to the first nonlosing record in franchise history at 8–8. In 2000, in his second year, Baltimore finished the regular season with a 12–4 record, and rolled through the play-offs with a record-setting defense, winning Super Bowl XXXV.

Since his Super Bowl win, Billick has been one of the league's more high-profile coaches, making frequent television appearances as a commentator and guest.

NICK BOLLETTIERI— AN ACE OF A COACH

Birth date: July 31, 1931

Birthplace: North Pelham, New York

Claim to fame: Founded the Nick Bollettieri Tennis Academy, the world's first full-time tennis school.

Appropriate quote about Bollettieri: "Everyone there [at Bollettieri's Tennis Academy] is just very dedicated. They're working all the time, and that's a good environment to be in if you want to be a professional athlete."

—Miles Kasiri, tennis player

Nick Bollettieri is a tennis maverick who revolutionized the way tennis and sports are taught in the United States and across the globe. In 1977, he founded the Nick Bollettieri Tennis Academy (NBTA), training junior tennis players on weekends for $35 per session. He was so successful that a year later he began offering students a full-time curriculum along with room and board.

In 1980, NBTA ballooned to 200 students, with a facility that included 22 tennis courts and 32 condominiums. It became a magnet for tennis prodigies and consistently developed world-class players. At its peak in 1987, NBTA boasted 32 students in the main draw at Wimbledon, and 27 students in the U.S. Open.

That year, Bollettieri sold his academy to International Management Group (IMG), the largest sports management company in the world. Bollettieri stayed on as the academy's president and driving force, and with IMG's financial backing NBTA continued to expand. In 1994, it became the Bollettieri Sports Academy, offering Nick's unique philosophy and training program in a variety of sports in addition to tennis, including golf, soccer, hockey, and baseball. It is the largest such academy in the world.

Nick Bollettieri has trained some of tennis's greatest players, including Andre Agassi, Jim Courier, Monica Seles, Boris Becker, and Maria Sharapova.

In 2002, Bollettieri was inducted into the Italian American Sports Hall of Fame.

BOBBY BOWDEN—SOUTHERN FRIED WINNER

Birth date: November 8, 1929
Birthplace: Birmingham, Alabama

Claim to fame: Winningest coach in Division I college football history
Appropriate quote about Bowden: "When he says, 'This is how I
would have done it,' you get the message that that's the way you
better do it. And when it's over, it's over. When you walk out that
door, he'll say, 'OK, buddy, let's go get 'em.'"

—FSU assistant coach Darrell Mudra

Teams expecting southern hospitality are in for a rude awakening
when they visit the Florida State Seminoles in Tallahassee. For the
past twenty years the 'Noles have been one of the most dominant
college football programs in the nation, and Bowden's coaching legend has become folklore in the tradition-rich South.

In his youth, Bowden lived across the street from the high school
football field where he would become a star quarterback in his teens.
In college, he played one year of football at the University of
Alabama, then returned home to Birmingham. He got married and
played for Howard College (now Samford University), earning small-
college All-American recognition as a quarterback.

After his playing career ended, he paid his dues as a coach, working at several assistant-coaching jobs before becoming the head
coach at Howard in 1959. He coached Howard to a record of 31–6
over four years, then moved on to assistant-coaching jobs at Florida
State and West Virginia University. In 1970, Bowden became head
coach at West Virginia and over the next six years he guided the
Mountaineers to a 42–26 record and two bowl game appearances.

In 1976 he finally found a permanent home. He took over a
Florida State program that was in shambles, having won only four
games in the previous three years. After a 5–6 record in his first year,
he has never had another losing season. The team went 10–2 in his
second year and earned a postseason bowl berth. Since 1982 he has
led the Seminoles to a bowl game every season, eleven straight bowl
wins (1985–95), and two national championships, in 1993 and 1999.
Under Bowden's guidance, Florida State has become a college foot-

ball powerhouse, attracting the best athletes from across the country. It is a feared stop on the schedule of any opponent.

Bobby Bowden's success at Florida State ranks among the greatest achievements in the history of the sport. He is the winningest coach in Division I college football history, just ahead of fellow coaching legend Joe Paterno of Penn State. He is the only coach in Division I to compile thirteen straight ten-win seasons, and has coached such standout players as Deion Sanders, Derrick Brooks, and Charlie Ward. Bowden was named ACC Coach of the Year in 1993 and 1997.

SCOTTY BOWMAN—
THE GREATEST COACH ON ICE

Birth date: September 18, 1933
Birthplace: Montreal, Quebec, Canada
Claim to fame: Winner of nine Stanley Cups with three different teams
Appropriate quote about Bowman: "He doesn't accept mediocrity, and he's instilled that in us."
>   —*Darren McCarty, former Detroit Red Wings forward*

Scotty Bowman is a true success story of perseverance, determination, and grit. Undoubtedly the most successful coach in the history of the NHL, he is ranked first in wins, playoff wins, and (most importantly) Stanley Cup victories, with nine. Bowman has coached many of the greatest players the league has ever seen, including Guy Lafleur, Bob Gainey, Gilbert Perreault, Steve Yzerman, Dominik Hasek, and Mario Lemieux. Amazingly, his nine Stanley Cups have come with three different teams: Montreal (1973, 1976–79), Pittsburgh (1992), and Detroit (1997, 1998, and 2002).

Bowman grew up with hockey in his blood. As a young boy in his native Montreal, he listened to games on the radio and aspired to play in the NHL one day. He made it to the Canadiens' junior team, but after suffering a career-ending head injury during a game, he was forced to give up playing the sport he loved. Ironically this injury benefited Bowman as a coach, allowing him to begin coaching at a younger age than most men in his new profession.

He soaked up the game and early in his career became known as a persistent tactician. He broke into the NHL as a head coach in 1966 with the first-year expansion St. Louis Blues. In his first three seasons with the Blues, Bowman's team was swept in the Stanley Cup Finals, losing three finals in a row. Since those early disappointments, he has won nine of the next ten finals in which he has appeared.

In thirty years of coaching, Bowman had a 1244–583–314 mark in the regular season and was 223–130 in the play-offs. He holds NHL records for wins, winning percentage (.654), play-off games coached, and play-off victories. He won the Jack Adams Award as coach of the year in 1977 and 1996, and he was named NHL executive of the year in 1980.

JOHN CHANEY—PERENNIAL OVERACHIEVER

Birth date: January 21, 1932
Birthplace: Jacksonville, Florida
Claim to fame: Creator of trapping matchup zone defense designed to slow down games and play to his team's strengths
Appropriate quote about Chaney: "Coach is like the father figure that most of us don't have."

—*Kevin Lyde, former Temple center*

John Chaney is a Philadelphia institution. He is as famous for his passionate sideline tirades as he is for taking many underprivileged student-athletes and molding them into winners. Since becoming the men's head basketball coach of the Temple Owls in 1982, he resurrected the program, leading them to twenty postseason appearances in twenty-one years and a total of eighteen NCAA tournament appearances.

Temple's matchup zone defense is a Chaney trademark and made the Owls a dangerous opponent for any team that faced them in the one-game elimination NCAA Tournament. By forming disciplined, trapping units, they frustrated more talented squads into playing the Owls' slower-paced style. "Defense at Temple is what offense was to the Lakers back in Magic Johnson's day," basketball coach Mark Schmidt once said.

Before going to Temple, Chaney coached Cheyney State for ten years, beginning in 1972. During his tenure, Cheyney State became a national Division II power, compiling a remarkable record of 225–59 for a winning percentage of .792. In 1978, Cheyney State won the Division II National Championship and coach Chaney won National Coach of the Year honors.

Chaney led the Owls to five NCAA Regional Finals, with six Atlantic 10 championships and eight Atlantic 10 regular season titles. He was named Atlantic 10 Conference Coach of the Year five times. He compiled fifteen twenty-win seasons and ranks fifth all-time in most twenty-win seasons. He is the winningest coach in Atlantic 10 history.

In 2002, John Chaney was enshrined in the National Basketball Hall of Fame with Duke coach Mike Krzyzewski and NBA great Moses Malone. Following the 2006 season, Coach Chaney retired from Temple, culminating a lifetime dedicated to the sport he loves.

BILL COWHER—MAN OF STEEL

Birth date: May 8, 1957

Birthplace: Pittsburgh, Pennsylvania

Claim to fame: Fiery, Super Bowl–winning head coach of the Pittsburgh Steelers

Appropriate quote about Cowher: "He's mellowed some, but in ways that effect the team, he hasn't changed one bit. He's as fiery as he's always been. As a player, you feed off it."

—*former Steelers running back Jerome Bettis*

Bill Cowher was born to coach the Steelers and is as synonymous with Pittsburgh as U.S. Steel is. A former linebacker and special teams standout, Cowher looks the part of a football renegade, sometimes appearing as though he would still like to run on the field himself and get in on the action. He is emotional on the sidelines and can often be seen engaging in animated discussions with players and referees. His distinctive mustache and powerful jawline mirror his forceful personality.

Cowher grew up in the Steel City, and excelled in football, basketball, and track. He attended Carlynton High in Crafton, Pennsylvania, a suburb of Pittsburgh. After high school, he became a starting linebacker for North Carolina State University, and then the team's captain and MVP in his senior year. Cowher graduated in 1979.

As a player, he signed as a free agent with the Philadelphia Eagles in 1979, was cut, and then signed with the Cleveland Browns the following year. He played three seasons (1980–82) in Cleveland before being traded back to the Eagles, where he played two more years (1983–84). During his playing career he displayed the fiery competitiveness and hard-nosed determination that would later make him a terrific coach.

Cowher's coaching career began in 1985 as an assistant to head coach Marty Schottenheimer with the Cleveland Browns. He was Cleveland's special teams coach in 1985–86 and secondary coach in 1987–88. When Schottenheimer left the Browns in 1989, Cowher followed him to Kansas City, and was promoted to defensive coordinator.

In 1992, at the age of thirty-five, he got his break, becoming one of the youngest head coaches in league history. Cowher took the Steelers to the play-offs in his first six seasons at the helm. They reached the Super Bowl in 1995, but lost to the Dallas Cowboys. Cowher earned Coach of the Year honors in 1992 and 2004, and ranks ninth in NFL history for longest head coaching service with one team. In 2006, he led the Steelers to their fifth Super Bowl title.

Despite his fiery personality and volatile intensity, Cowher's head coaching record is a model of consistency. He has been with the Steelers since his hiring—the longest active tenure of any head coach in the NFL—and has carried on their tradition of rugged power football.

ANNE DONOVAN—TOWER OF CONSISTENCY

Birth date: November 1, 1961
Birthplace: Ridgewood, New Jersey
Claim to fame: First female coach to win the WNBA championship
Appropriate quote about Donovan: "Anne Donovan is an accomplished head coach, an excellent communicator, a student of the game, and a great spokesperson for women's basketball."
　　　　　　　　　—*Billy McKinney, Seattle Storm general manager*

At six foot eight, Anne Donovan was a force to be reckoned with as a player. Now, as she strolls the sidelines in the WNBA, she's become an intimidating presence again, known to coach hardworking teams with a suffocating defense.

In high school, Donovan was unstoppable, averaging thirty-five points and seventeen rebounds a game in 1979. She led Paramus Catholic to two straight undefeated seasons and two straight Group III state championships, in 1978 and 1979.

Then, from 1979 to 1983, she was one of the most dominant college players that women's basketball has ever seen. At center for Old Dominion University, she averaged a double-double (20 points and 14.5 rebounds) for her college career, and was an intimidating shot-blocker.

Multiskilled under the basket, Donovan could carry a team on her back. In her first year with Old Dominion, she led the team to a remarkable 37–1 record and the 1979 AIAW National Championship. In 1983, she took the team to the NCAA Final Four, and ended her career at Old Dominion as the Lady Monarchs' all-time leading scorer (2,719 points), rebounder (1,976), and shot-blocker (801).

After college, she went on to an illustrious professional career. As an Olympian, she won gold medals with the U.S. team in 1984 and 1988, and world championships in 1983 and 1986. She also played professionally for five years in Japan and one year in Italy, before she returned to the United States and began her coaching career.

As a coach, Donovan is an experienced winner. She started as an assistant at her alma mater, Old Dominion (1989–95), before becoming head coach at East Carolina University (1995–98). She also served as an assistant coach on two U.S. world championship teams, in 1998 and 2002.

In 2001, Donovan took over as head coach of the WNBA's Charlotte Sting. After starting the season 1–10, she turned the team around, leading Charlotte to the WNBA Finals. She coached the Sting for two seasons before being named head coach of the Seattle Storm in 2002.

Anne Donovan made history in 2004 as the first female coach to lead her team to the WNBA Championship when the Storm beat the Connecticut Sun two games to one in the finals.

Anne Donovan was enshrined in the Basketball Hall of Fame as a player on May 15, 1995.

ANGELO DUNDEE—TRAINER OF CHAMPIONS

Birth date: August 30, 1921

Birthplace: Philadelphia, Pennsylvania

Claim to fame: Hall of Fame boxing trainer of Muhammad Ali and Sugar Ray Leonard

Appropriate quote about Dundee: "He is the only man in boxing to whom I would entrust my own son."

—*Sportscaster Howard Cosell*

He looks and speaks like the neighborhood grocery-store vendor, but don't be fooled. Underneath his unassuming exterior Angelo Dundee is a master motivator and one of the greatest boxing trainers of the twentieth century. He has trained fifteen world champions, including boxing legends Muhammad Ali, Sugar Ray Leonard, and George Foreman.

A self-described "old school" trainer, Dundee studied the art of working a corner at New York's famed Stillman's Gym in the 1940s, working with or studying Al Goldman, Chickie Ferrera, Freddie Brown, and Ray Arcel. He took bits and pieces from each, molding the different styles into his own unique approach that he refers to as "Dundeeism."

During the 1950s, Dundee moved to Miami and became the head trainer of the soon-to-be-world-famous Fifth Street Gym. Here, along with Chris, his brother and a promoter, he trained and managed a stable of some of the world's best fighters. He established himself as one of the best and most honorable cornermen in the business. As his reputation for skill and character grew, he was sought out by some of the top talent in the boxing world.

In 1960 he was tapped to train a young, brash heavyweight named Cassius Clay. Over the next twenty years, he guided Clay (who later changed his name to Muhammad Ali) in some of boxing's greatest fights. Dundee trained Ali to throw punches in rapid combinations and flurries, culminating with a signature overhand right knockout finish. Dundee and Ali formed the most well-known trainer-fighter tandem in the history of the sport, and under Dundee's guidance Ali won the heavyweight title an unprecedented three times.

In 1976, Sugar Ray Leonard was America's boxing Golden Boy, having just won Olympic gold in the games at Montreal. Leonard's trainers summoned the now-legendary Dundee to mold their young fighter into a champion. Three years later, Leonard and Dundee accomplished their mission as Leonard captured his first world title, defeating Wilfredo Benitez by TKO in the fifteenth round.

Dundee has been the chief cornerman in some of the most famous fights in boxing history, including the Fight of the Century (Ali-Frazier I), the Rumble in the Jungle (Ali-Foreman), the Thrilla in Manila (Ali-Frazier III), Leonard-Duran I and II, and Leonard-Hearns I.

The Boxing Writers Association of America named Dundee its Manager of the Year in 1968 and 1979. He was also awarded the organization's Long and Meritorious Service Award in 1996. Angelo Dundee was elected to the International Boxing Hall of Fame in 1994.

TONY DUNGY—QUIET CONFIDENCE

Birth date: October 6, 1955
Birthplace: Jackson, Michigan
Claim to fame: Intelligent, defensive-minded football coach
Appropriate quote about Dungy: "In this league, with dogs and people stabbing you in the back and all the things he's been through, he's still looked upon as a good man with integrity. That's so admirable."
　　　　　　　　　　　　　　　—Tarik Glenn, Indianapolis Colts tackle

Tony Dungy's football intellect was developed while playing a variety of positions, from quarterback to wide receiver to safety, and becoming an assistant coach in the NFL at the tender age of twenty-five.

Dungy attended the University of Minnesota and quarterbacked the Golden Gophers from 1973 to 1976, earning team MVP honors twice. He finished his collegiate career as the career leader in a number of offensive categories.

In May 1977, he signed as a free agent with the Pittsburgh Steelers and they converted him from quarterback to safety. He played two seasons with Pittsburgh, including their 1978 world championship team, and connected with head coach Chuck Knoll, who would become one of Dungy's mentors. After the Super Bowl season, Pittsburgh traded Dungy to San Francisco, where he played the 1979 season.

In 1980, Dungy began his coaching career as defensive backs coach at his alma mater, the University of Minnesota. The following season, he returned to the NFL and coached under Knoll as an assistant defensive coach with the Steelers. In 1984, he was promoted to Steelers defensive coordinator and began to make a name for himself as one of the league's sharpest defensive minds.

He served as an assistant coach and defensive coordinator for the next twelve years with the Steelers, Kansas City Chiefs, and Minnesota Vikings. In 1996, he got his first head coaching opportunity with the league's worst franchise, the Tampa Bay Bucaneers.

He quickly turned the Buccaneers from a perennial cellar dweller to an NFL powerhouse. In his second season, they finished 10–6 and made the play-offs. In 1999, he took them to within one game of the Super Bowl. Under Dungy, the Tampa Bay defense became one of the strongest units in the league, boasting All-Pros Warren Sapp, Derrick Brooks, and John Lynch. During this period, however, the offense struggled, particularly in the play-offs, and Dungy was fired following the 2001 season. Some thought the firing unjust and a bit premature considering the team's turnaround. Dungy was the most successful head coach in franchise history, compiling a 54–42 regular season record and earning four play-off appearances in six seasons.

In 2002, the season following Dungy's departure, Tampa Bay won the Super Bowl with John Gruden coaching a team assembled primarily by Dungy. Typical of Coach Dungy's quiet, respectful personality, he said nothing negative about his firing or the Bucs' Super Bowl win.

Within forty-eight hours of being let go by Tampa, Dungy was contacted by Indianapolis Colts owner Robert Irsay and offered the head coaching job. Coach Dungy accepted and has been coaching the Colts since 2002. Under his guidance, they have not had a losing season, and reached the AFC Championship game in 2003. The Colts, in contrast to the Buccaneers, possess a lethal offense, with quarterback Peyton Manning and wide receiver Marvin Harrison.

HERMAN EDWARDS—
MIRACLE IN THE MEADOWLANDS

Birthdate: April 27, 1954
Birthplace: Eatontown, New Jersey (Fort Monmouth Army Base)
Claim to fame: Recovered fumble for "Miracle in the Meadowlands"
Appropriate quote about Edwards: "Herm cares about his players.
He'll go to bat for you, as long as you work hard for him."

— *Jason Ferguson, Jets nose tackle*

On November 19, 1978, one of the most memorable plays in NFL
history occurred. With only twenty seconds left in the game, Herman
Edwards of the Philadelphia Eagles picked up a fumble by New York
Giants quarterback Joe Pisarcik, and sprinted twenty-six yards into
the end zone, giving the Eagles the victory and a play-off berth. The
play, dubbed "the Miracle in the Meadowlands," is symbolic of Herman Edwards's NFL career—a long shot.

Edwards played at three different colleges: the University of California, Berkeley; Monterey Peninsula Junior College; and his senior
season at San Diego State. He was undrafted and made the Philadelphia Eagles as a free agent in 1978. He played ten seasons in the
NFL, appearing with Philadelphia in the 1980 Super Bowl, and making second team All-NFC honors in 1980 and 1982.

Edwards retired in 1986, and began his coaching career as defensive backs coach at San Jose State from 1987 to 1989. In 1990,
Edwards joined the NFL's Kansas City Chiefs staff, assisting then
defensive backs coach Tony Dungy. He coached at Kansas City until
1996, leaving with Dungy when Dungy was hired as head coach of
the Tampa Bay Buccaneers.

In Tampa, Edwards was defensive backfield coach and assistant
head coach. He worked closely with Tampa free safety John Lynch,
molding him into an All-Pro. The Tampa defense became one of the

NFL's best, and the Buccaneers became a Super Bowl contender during Edwards's tenure.

In 2001, after five solid seasons in Tampa Bay, Herman Edwards became head coach of the New York Jets. He guided the Jets to the play-offs in his first two seasons, winning the AFC East in 2002. In 2004, he again led the Jets to the play-offs despite the loss of starting quarterback and franchise player Chad Pennington.

Following the 2005 season, Coach Edwards left New York to take over as head coach of the Kansas City Chiefs. Edwards is known as one of the league's most impassioned motivators.

JEFF FISHER—COACH OF THE TITANS

Birth date: February 25, 1958
Birthplace: Culver City, California
Claim to fame: Bright, defensive-minded coach of the Tennessee Titans
Appropriate quote about Fisher: "You can't do anything but believe in
    the guy because he's still fighting. And you know you've got to
    believe in a fighter."

—former Titans linebacker Barron Wortham

Jeff Fisher is a southern California native with a football pedigree. He was a high school All-American at Toreadors of Taft High School in Woodland Hills. Fisher then attended college at USC from 1977 to 1980, playing defensive back in a star-studded Trojans secondary that included future NFL stars Joey Browner, Dennis Smith, and Ronnie Lott. He was a member of USC's 1978 national championship team.

In 1981 Fisher was drafted in the seventh round by the Chicago Bears, and played five seasons in the NFL as a defensive back and return specialist. In 1985, Fisher, on injured reserve after suffering a career-ending ankle injury, assisted Bears defensive coordinator

Buddy Ryan with the dominating defense that propelled Chicago to their 1985 Super Bowl win.

Fisher officially began his coaching career in 1986 as a defensive backs coach under Ryan, who left Chicago to become head coach of the Philadelphia Eagles. In 1988, he became the league's youngest defensive coordinator, overseeing an Eagles unit that led the league in sacks and interceptions in 1989. In 1990, the Philly D led the league in rushing defense and was second in sacks.

In 1994, Fisher joined the Houston Oilers coaching staff and replaced Jack Pardee as head coach later that season, becoming one of the NFL's youngest head coaches. The Oilers were a franchise in transition and, after moving to Tennessee in 1996, changed their name to the Tennessee Titans.

The move to Tennessee and Fisher's steady coaching solidified the franchise and the Titans became one of pro football's consistent winners. Tennessee made the play-offs in 1999, 2000, 2002, and 2003. They won division titles in 2000 and 2002, and in 1999 made it all the way to the Super Bowl, losing on the game's final play. They played in two AFC Championship games, in 1999 and 2002.

DAN GABLE—MASTER OF THE MAT

Birth date: October 25, 1948

Birthplace: Waterloo, Iowa

Claim to fame: Led University of Iowa to fifteen NCAA wrestling championships

Appropriate quote about Gable: "In my eyes, Dan Gable is one of the best coaches ever in any sport. He's relentless. I've seen other schools wrestle, and it's like a half-court game. Not Dan. It's exciting, attacking all over the mat—like a transition game."

—*University of Iowa women's basketball coach Angie Lee*

Dan Gable's luminous reputation is such that he has been referred to as the Babe Ruth of wrestling. A living legend in his native Iowa, he is by far the most well-known and respected figure wrestling has ever seen, possessing an almost superhuman drive to succeed.

At Waterloo West High School, he went undefeated from 1963 to 1966. After graduation, he attended Iowa State University, where he compiled a near flawless 118–1 record as a collegiate wrestler, winning NCAA titles in 1968 and 1969.

After college, Gable wrestled as an amateur and began preparing for the 1972 Olympics. His obsession to defeat the Russian team was so intense that he turned down an invitation to the White House prior to the Olympics because the trip would interrupt his training regimen.

His discipline paid off. At the 1972 Olympics in Munich, Gable, at 149 pounds, dominated and won the gold medal. After the games, he continued wrestling until retiring in 1973.

In 1976, Gable became the head wrestling coach at the University of Iowa, and began one of the most successful tenures of any coach in any sport. From 1978 to 1986, he led the Hawkeyes to nine consecutive NCAA titles, and a total of fifteen titles in twenty-one years as head coach.

He is the all-time winningest coach in Iowa's history, with a career record of 355–21–5, and has coached 152 All-Americans, 106 Big Ten champions, and 45 national champions.

He also coached the U.S. Olympic team in 1980, 1984, and 2000. The 1984 team, which featured four Iowa Hawkeyes, won seven gold medals. Gable also coached the World Cup team to three gold medals, and in June 2002 he was appointed to the President's Council on Physical Fitness and Sport.

Gable has been inducted into both the Olympic Hall of Fame and the National Wrestling Hall of Fame. In 1996, he was listed as one of the top one hundred U.S. Olympians of all time.

BRAD GILBERT—TENNIS GURU

Birth date: September 8, 1961

Birthplace: Oakland, California

Claim to fame: Turned Andre Agassi's career around

Appropriate quote about Gilbert: "What Brad helped me with the most was the ability to believe in myself by learning to think for myself. A great coach can lead you to a place where you don't need him anymore. Brad Gilbert is a great coach."

          —*Tennis great Andre Agassi*

In 1980 Brad Gilbert, a five-foot-eight, 130-pound college tennis player, had more confidence than experience. At Foothills Junior College in Los Altos Hills, California, his coach, Tom Chivington, taught him to strengthen his game by improving his work ethic and strategy, thus enabling him to compete better. Now Gilbert is a coach who brings out the best in his players by accenting their strengths and exploiting their opponents' weaknesses.

He turned pro in 1981 and through the 1980s worked his way up the rankings, beating some of the world's top players, including Boris Becker, Jimmy Connors, and Stefan Edberg. Though not the most physically gifted player, he was known for his scrappiness and developed an uncanny knack for getting under an opponent's skin and inside their heads. He rose as high as number four in the world in 1990, and won a bronze medal at the 1988 Olympics.

In 1994, Andre Agassi had slumped to number 141 in the world and his career was heading south. Agassi needed a change and turned to Gilbert, who helped him refocus and make one of the greatest comebacks in tennis history. Agassi revitalized his career, won six Grand Slam titles, an Olympic gold medal, and reached the world's number-one ranking in 1999, all under Gilbert's tutelage. In 2002, the pair parted ways amicably.

In 2003, another talented young American, Andy Roddick, turned to Gilbert, who immediately instilled confidence in the gifted prodigy. Roddick won the 2003 U.S. Open and captured the world's number-one ranking at the end of 2003.

After parting ways with Roddick in 2004, Gilbert continues to work with tennis's top players at his home in San Rafael, California, and is a familiar face on the tennis tour, making frequent television and radio appearances.

CARRIE GRAF—A WINNER FROM DOWN UNDER

Claim to fame: Famed Australian basketball player and coach

Appropriate quote about Graf: "I know what I can expect with her as a head coach. She is a very enthusiastic person when it comes to the game of basketball, and her coaching credentials in Australia really speak for themselves."

—*Kayte Christensen, Phoenix Mercury forward*

Carrie Graf hails from down under and is an experienced winner in international basketball competition as both a player and coach. She played professionally from 1983 to 1990 with the WNBL's Nunawading Spectres, earning Rookie of the Year honors in the Australian club championships in 1983, and making the under-eighteen All-Australian squad in 1984. She won five WNBL titles with the Spectres.

After her playing career ended, Graf worked double duty as a coach, in both her native Australia and the United States. She served as an assistant in the WNBA, with the Phoenix Mercury in 1998, 1999, 2001, and 2003.

She continued on as head coach of the WNBL's Sydney Flames from 1993 to 1996—during the WNBA's off-seasons—and the Canberra Capitals from 2000 to 2002, leading the Capitals to the WNBL championship in 2000 and 2002. Graf was also an assistant coach on the Australian National Team, which won the silver medal at the 2000 Olympics.

In 2004, she was named head coach of the WNBA's Phoenix Mercury, where she coached for two seasons, before stepping down in 2005. Graf is expected to head back to Australia to again take over as head coach of the Canberra Capitals. In seven seasons as a WNBL head coach, she posted a record of 119–29, with two championships.

Carrie Graf received the High Performance Coach Award in 1996 and the Young Coach of the Year Award in 1993 and 1996 from the Australian Coaching Council. She has a degree in physical education from RMIT in Melbourne, where she graduated in 1991, and resides in Sydney, Australia.

APRIL HEINRICHS—SOCCER PIONEER

Birth date: February 27, 1964
Birthplace: Denver, Colorado
Claim to fame: Coached the 2004 U.S. Women's soccer team to the Olympic gold medal
Appropriate quote about Heinrichs: "She is an unbelievable leader, motivator, and tactician. As a former captain and world champion with the national team, April is a proven winner."

> —*Julie Foudy, former U.S. team cocaptain*

As a child, April Heinrichs loved soccer and developed a tenacious competitiveness that would eventually become her trademark as both a player and a coach. She pioneered women's soccer in the United States, gaining a reputation as a player who could outwork and outwill opponents.

After high school, she attended the University of North Carolina and joined fabled coach Anson Dorrance's women's soccer program. While at Chapel Hill, Heinrichs and the Tar Heels made four consecutive NCAA championship game appearances and the team won NCAA titles in 1983, 1984, and 1986.

Individually, Heinrichs was a standout, leaving an indelible mark on collegiate women's soccer. By the time she graduated in 1986, she had scored eighty-seven goals and posted fifty-one assists, leading UNC to an 85–3–2 record over four years. She was named National Player of the Year for NCAA Women's Soccer in 1984 and 1986, and became the first women's soccer player in school history to have her jersey (Number 2) retired.

After college, Heinrichs joined the U.S. National Team and helped bring women's soccer in the United States into national prominence. Her leadership and mental and physical toughness were unmatched. She was a tireless worker who, along with Michelle Akers and Carin Jennings, formed what became known as the "Triple Edged Sword." In 1991, the team won the first ever Women's World Championship.

Some observers believe Heinrichs is responsible for instilling the winning mentality in the U.S. Women's Soccer Team that began in the 1980s and still continues today.

As a coach, Heinrichs has also distinguished herself at the collegiate and professional levels. In college, she was head coach at Princeton, then at Maryland where she won ACC Coach of the Year honors in 1995. She moved on to the University of Virginia and led the Cavaliers to four NCAA play-off berths and a record of 52–27–7.

In January 2000, she was named head coach of the U.S. Women's National Team, becoming the first female to hold the position in the history of the program. In five years as head coach, Heinrichs led the team to a stellar 87–17–20 record, a .782 winning percentage. In 2004, she culminated her coaching career, leading stars Mia Hamm and Heather Mitts to the 2004 Olympic gold medal in Greece.

April Heinrichs's impact on women's soccer in the United States has been incredible. In 1986 and 1989, she was named U.S. Soccer Federation Player of the Year, and was voted "Female Player of the

1980s" by *Soccer America* magazine. In 1998, she became the first female player inducted into the National Soccer Hall of Fame.

DORRELL NORMAN "WHITEY" HERZOG— THE WHITE RAT

Birth date: November 9, 1931
Birthplace: New Athens, Ilinois
Claim to fame: Managed 1982 St. Louis Cardinals to World Series victory
Appropriate quote about Herzog: "Every game is like a chess match with Whitey, and other managers must feel like they are playing against ten guys when they go up against him."

—*Columnist Larry King*

St. Louis is a true baseball town and Whitey Herzog is one of its favorite sons. In the 1980s he returned to his hometown and came into his own as a manger, rebuilding the proud Cardinals franchise with strong pitching, blazing speed, and wily managing.

As a player, Herzog had a mediocre eight-year career with the Washington Senators (1956–58), Kansas City Athletics (1958–60), Baltimore Orioles (1961–62), and Detroit Tigers (1963). He finished his career with a batting average of .257, with 25 home runs and 172 RBIs. He once quipped, "Baseball has been good to me since I quit playing it."

Herzog began managing on the professional level with the Texas Rangers in 1973, and then moved to the California Angels in 1974. In 1975, he took over as manager of the Kansas City Royals, leading them to three straight division titles, in 1976, 1977, and 1978. The Royals featured Hall of Fame third baseman George Brett.

In 1980, he moved to St. Louis, where he enjoyed his greatest success. He built his team with players like Hall of Fame shortstop Ozzie Smith, MVP Willie McGee, talented right-handed pitcher Joaquin

Andujar, and rock-solid second baseman Tommy Herr. The Cardinals were a balanced team, with a rare combination of just the right amounts of speed, power, brains, and cohesiveness. They won three National League pennants, in 1982, 1985, and 1987, winning the World Series in 1982. Whitey Herzog was voted Manager of the Year in 1985.

KEN HITCHCOCK—A HISTORY OF WINNING

Birth date: December 17, 1951
Birthplace: Edmonton, Alberta, Canada
Claim to fame: Stanley Cup–winning head coach of the 1998–99 Dallas Stars
Appropriate quote about Hitchcock: "Coach Hitchcock is widely regarded as one of the top hockey coaches in the world."
　　　　　　　　　—Princeton University hockey coach Guy Gadowsky

He's known around the league as Hitch, and is one of hockey's most friendly and knowledgeable coaches. Hitch has a way with people; he makes you feel comfortable and is an articulate conversationalist with a broad variety of interests.

His coaching career began in 1984 with the Kamloops Blazers of the Western Hockey League. He enjoyed tremendous success with the Blazers over six seasons, winning the WHL championship in 1985–86 and 1989–90, and being named Canadian Junior Hockey Coach of the Year in 1990. He never had a losing season in the WHL.

In 1990, he joined the NHL's Philadelphia Flyers as an assistant for three seasons before leaving to become the head coach of the Dallas Stars' IHL team, the Kalamazoo Wings, for the 1993–94 season. In 1996 he was named head coach of the Dallas Stars in the NHL.

Dallas made it to the conference finals in 1997–98, and Hitchcock was named as a coach in the NHL All-Star Game, the first of three successive appearances. In 1998–99, Coach Hitchcock guided the Dallas Stars to their first and only Stanley Cup championship.

They reached the Finals again in 1999–2000, losing the Cup to the New Jersey Devils in six games.

In 2002, Hitchcock took over as head coach of the Philadelphia Flyers and led them to the play-offs in his first season. In 2003–04, the Flyers made it to the Eastern Conference Finals before losing to eventual champion Tampa Bay in seven games.

BELA KAROLYI—A PERFECT 10 OF A COACH

Birth date: September 13, 1942
Birthplace: Cluj-Napoca, Romania
Claim to fame: World's most famous and successful gymnastics coach
Appropriate quote about Karolyi: "It's not by accident that Bela is who he is and has accomplished what he has. It's by very, very hard work and that's what he instills in all of us. Work."
—*Kathy Kelly, U.S. women's gymnastics program director*

As coach, Karolyi is known as a taskmaster, a driving force imploring his young pupils to succeed. He has drawn criticism for this, from both inside and outside the sport. His students, however, see it differently. "Bela is a consummate perfectionist, who puts himself on the line for the good of his athletes," says Betty Okino.

In 1970s, Karolyi built the Romanian National Gymnastics Team into a world power, peaking with Nadia Comaneci's famed performance at the 1976 Olympic Games in Montreal. In 1981, he defected to the United States and soon added to his legend by raising the United States gymnastics program to the same elite level.

Bela Karolyi's coaching efforts have produced twenty-eight Olympians, nine Olympic champions, fifteen world champions, twelve European medalists, and six U.S. national champions in his thirty-year career in both his native Romania and the United States. Among his most accomplished gymnasts are Nadia Comaneci, Mary Lou Retton, Kim Zmeskal, Betty Okino, Kerri Strug, and Dominique

Moceanu. In 1997, he was inducted into the International Gymnastics Hall of Fame.

TRUDI LACEY—BELIEVE IN YOURSELF

Claim to fame: Head coach and general manager of the WNBA's Charlotte Sting

Appropriate quote about Lacey: "Trudi is a proven leader with a great mind for the game and a winning rapport with her players and staff."
—*Ed Tapscott, CEO, Charlotte Bobcats and Sting*

Trudi Lacey was a star basketball player at North Carolina State University, and was named an All-American in 1980. She was the team's MVP twice and was a four-time All–AIAW Tournament selection.

Lacey began her coaching career as an assistant with Manhattan College in 1981, then coached at James Madison (1982) and North Carolina State (1983–84). In 1986, she got her first head coaching job with Francis Marion (1986–88). In 1988, she took over as head coach at the University of South Florida, coaching there through 1996.

In 1997, Lacey joined USA Basketball as an assistant coach, helping develop the women's team that won the gold medal at the 2000 Olympic Games in Sydney, Australia.

In 2001, Lacey became an assistant coach with the WNBA's Charlotte Sting, and helped the Sting advance to the play-offs in 2001 and 2002. In 2003, she was promoted to head coach and general manager, overseeing the Sting's basketball operations on and off the court. She coached the Sting until 2005, when she stepped down as head coach, but remained with the team as general manager.

MARVIN LEWIS—HARD HITTER

Birth date: September 23, 1958
Birthplace: McDonald, Pennsylvania

Claim to fame: Defensive coordinator of 2000 Super Bowl champion Baltimore Ravens

Appropriate quote about Lewis: "It's all due to Marvin Lewis. He completely turned this ball club around. He taught us everything, from how to practice, how to lift, how to study tape, and all the little things . . . eat right, get your rest. Stuff that we never used to do before he brought here, and everyone bought into his system."

—Bengals wide receiver Chad Johnson

Marvin Lewis coaches with the aggressive, hard-hitting mentality of a linebacker, the position he played at Iowa State from 1978 to 1980, earning All–Big Sky Conference honors in those seasons.

Lewis began his coaching career at Idaho State in 1981, earning a degree in physical education in 1981 and a master's in athletic administration in 1982. In 1985, he moved on to become linebackers coach at Long Beach State (1985–86), New Mexico (1987–89), and Pittsburgh (1990–91).

In 1992, he moved to the NFL as linebackers coach with the Pittsburgh Steelers, where he helped develop defensive standouts Kevin Greene, Levon Kirkland, and Gregg Lloyd. The Steelers made the Super Bowl in 1995, and the following year, Lewis was hired as defensive coordinator of the Baltimore Ravens.

From 1996 to 2001, while with the Ravens, Lewis put together one of the NFL's all-time best defenses. In 2000, the Ravens' defense dominated the league en route to a Super Bowl championship. They shut out four opponents during the regular season, the most shutouts in the NFL since 1976, and allowed only 970 rushing yards all year—an NFL record.

In 2003, Lewis was hired as head coach of the Cincinnati Bengals, one of the league's worst teams. In his first year, the Bengals were the NFL's most improved team, six games better than the previous season, finishing the year at 8–8. It was the Bengals' first nonlosing season in seven years. In 2005, he guided the Bengals to their first winning season in twenty-five years.

LUTE OLSON—THE SILVER FOX

Birth date: September 22, 1934

Birthplace: Mayville, North Dakota

Claim to fame: Hall of Fame basketball coach of the University of Arizona

Appropriate quote about Olson: "He was a father figure that always had his office open and time to talk."

—*Chris Mills, former University of Arizona forward*

With his impeccable suits, rigid posture, and shining white hair, Lute Olson looks like he could be the president of the United States. He's been manning the sidelines on college basketball courts for over thirty years and has compiled an impeccable résumé to match his stylish appearance.

He started playing in the fifth grade and led his high school team in Grand Forks, North Dakota, to the 1952 state basketball championship. Olson then attended college at Augsburg, in Minnesota, from 1953 to 1956, where he played basketball, football, and baseball.

After graduation, he coached at the high school level in Minnesota for five years, then moved to California where he coached high schools in Anaheim and Huntington Beach for six years. During his eleven years as a high school coach, he put together a record of 180–76, for a .703 winning percentage.

In 1969, Olson moved to Long Beach State Junior College, guiding them to three league titles in his four seasons there. He became head coach of Long Beach State in 1973, and coached them to an impressive 24–2 record. The University of Iowa took notice and hired Olson to head their basketball program the next year.

Iowa had finished in last place in the Big Ten in 1973. In two years he turned the team around with a 19–10 record, and in 1978–79, Iowa made the NCAA tournament. The next year they made the tournament again, surviving to the Final Four. In his last five seasons with Iowa, Olson and his team made the NCAA tournament each year.

In 1983, he headed to the University of Arizona, where he has built one of the top programs in college basketball. Under Olson, the Wildcats have twenty consecutive NCAA tournament appearances, advanced to the Final Four four times, and won the national championship in 1997. He has also led Arizona to ten PAC-10 championships.

Lute Olson was enshrined in the Basketball Hall of Fame in 2002.

TOM OSBORNE—THE NEBRASKAN

Birth date: February 23, 1937
Birthplace: Hastings, Nebraska
Claim to fame: Three national championships as a coach
Appropriate quote about Osborne: "Tom Osborne is one of the good guys in coaching and in any profession. He's an icon in Nebraska and in this nation."

— *Bobby Bowden, legendary Florida State football coach*

Tom Osborne is a Midwesterner who epitomizes the strong, silent type. As head football coach of the Nebraska Cornhuskers, he was as steady as they come, and lets his record speak for itself.

Osborne graduated from Hastings College in Nebraska in 1959 as a star quarterback and basketball player. He played three seasons in the NFL—two with the Washington Redskins and one with the San Francisco 49ers.

In 1962, he joined Nebraska coach Bob Devaney's staff and worked under him for the next eleven years, being elevated to assistant head coach in 1972. He became head coach in 1973, a position he would hold for twenty-five years.

During his tenure, Nebraska won with an overwhelming ground attack, their straight-ahead style a direct reflection of their stubborn coach. They never won fewer than nine games in a season under Osborne and played in a bowl game every year he coached.

In the 1990s, after two decades of very good football but no national championships, Osborne and his Huskers finally broke through in sensational fashion. They went undefeated in 1994 and 1995 and won the national championship both years. In 1997, they made it three titles in four years by going undefeated again for the national title. From 1993 to 1997, they put together the best five-year record in NCAA history at 60–3.

Under Osborne, Nebraska boasted fifty-five All-Americans and forty-six Academic All-Americans. He coached such stars as Vince Ferragamo, Mike Rozier, and Tommie Frazier.

Coach Osborne retired from coaching after the 1997 season, and in 2000 he was elected to the United States Congress as a representative of his home state of Nebraska.

DUANE CHARLES "BILL" PARCELLS— THE BIG TUNA

Birth date: August 27, 1941

Birthplace: Englewood, New Jersey

Claim to fame: Two-time Super Bowl–winning coach of the New York Giants

Appropriate quote about Parcells: "When we were playing real well as a team, he was miserable because he needs friction. He lives on that friction. He needs adversity, and he's got to have a spat going with a player. If there's no adversity, he'll create it."

—former Giants quarterback Phil Simms

Parcells was born in Englewood, New Jersey, and grew up in nearby Oradell, where he attended River Dell High School in the mid-1950s. He was a big young man at six-foot-two and 180 pounds, and he excelled in football, baseball, and basketball.

After high school, Clemson and Auburn offered Parcells athletic scholarships, but he chose Colgate instead. He transferred to Wichita State after his freshman year, where he completed his collegiate studies and continued in athletics. As a senior linebacker, he played well enough to be named to the All–Missouri Valley Conference team, convincing the NFL's Detroit Lions to draft him in the seventh round in 1964. Two weeks into Detroit's exhibition season, however, they cut him, officially ending his playing career.

Parcells then bounced around the collegiate ranks, paying his dues as an assistant coach at a string of colleges including Hastings College, Wichita State, Army, Florida State, Vanderbilt, and Texas Tech. He served one season as the head coach at the Air Force Academy. In 1980, Parcells was offered the job of linebackers coach with the New England Patriots. He took the job and the next season moved to the New York Giants as defensive coordinator, under head coach Ray Perkins.

After the 1982 season, Ray Perkins stepped down and Parcells replaced him, earning his first head coaching job in the NFL. He wasn't an instant success, and in 1983, when the Giants went 3–12–1, he was almost fired.

In 1984, he asserted himself more as a coach, tapping Phil Simms as his starting quarterback and turning the team around. The Giants made it to the play-offs the next two seasons, but lost the divisional play-offs in successive years to San Francisco (in 1984) and Chicago (in 1985)—both Super Bowl winners.

Then, in 1986, Parcells's philosophy wore down the league. His ball-control offense and wrecking-ball defense were unstoppable. After losing the opening game to Dallas, the Giants went 17–1 the rest of the season. They crushed Joe Montana and the 49ers in the

NFC Championship Game 49–3, and then clobbered Denver 39–20 to win Super Bowl XXI. Parcells had climbed the highest of coaching's mountains. In 1990 he took the Giants to their second Super Bowl victory.

Parcells retired from coaching following the 1990 season for health reasons, but has returned to lead three different teams (New England, New York Jets, and Dallas Cowboys) to the play-offs, including a Super Bowl appearance with New England in 1996.

With two Super Bowl wins, and play-off appearances with four teams, Bill Parcells ranks among the best coaches in NFL history. He is one of four active coaches to have won at least two Super Bowls, and was the NFL's Coach of the Year in 1986 and 1989. He is a certain Hall of Famer when he retires.

MIKE SCIOSCIA—SOLID AS A ROCK

Birth date: November 27, 1958
Birthplace: Upper Darby Township, Pennsylvania
Claim to fame: Three-time World Series winner
Appropriate quote about Scioscia: "He's the best plate-blocking catcher
   I've seen in forty-six years of baseball."
                              —*Al Campanis, former Dodgers vice president*

Mike Scioscia has been playing and managing baseball on the West Coast for more than thirty years, but still employs the workmanlike philosophy instilled in him as a youth growing up just outside of Philadelphia.

Scioscia attended Springfield High School in Pennsylvania and was selected by the Los Angeles Dodgers in the first round (nineteenth overall) of the 1976 draft. After being called up in 1980, Scioscia enjoyed a stellar career with Los Angeles.

Scioscia was known for his ability to block home plate and handle a pitching staff. In 1988, he was a leader on the Dodgers' improbable World Series team. He hit a crucial, game-tying home run off Dwight Gooden in the ninth inning of Game 4 of the 1988 NLCS against New York. From 1980 to 1992, he played in 1,441 games with the Dodgers and ranks among team leaders in games caught, hits, and total bases. He was named to the National League All-Star team in 1989 and 1990.

In 1999 Scioscia became manager of the Anaheim Angels and has turned the team into a consistent winner ever since. His teams are known for executing fundamentals and playing "small ball," which involves stealing bases and bunting more frequently than most American League teams. Scioscia believes the little things put his team in the best position to win, especially in the play-offs when games tend to swing on one or two big plays.

In 2002, the Angels entered the play-offs as the wild card and were underdogs in each series they played. Scioscia kept his team focused "game to game" during their play-off run. First, they shocked the New York Yankees three games to one to advance to the American League Championship Series, where they made quick work of the Minnesota Twins, knocking them off four games to one to advance to the World Series. The Angels prevailed four games to three against Barry Bonds and the San Francisco Giants to win their first Series championship.

Scioscia was named 2002 Manager of the Year and led the Angels to the Western Division title in 2004 and 2005.

ORLANDO "TUBBY" SMITH— SMALL-TOWN BOY, BIG-TIME COACH

Birth date: June 30, 1951
Birthplace: Scotland, Maryland
Claim to fame: Coached the Kentucky Wildcats to 1998 NCAA Men's Basketball Championship

Appropriate quote about Smith: "Tubby has more integrity and honesty and class than any person I've found in this business."
—*University of Kentucky athletic director Mitch Barnhart*

Tubby Smith has been a leader since his playing days at High Point College in North Carolina. He was the team's captain in his senior year, graduating as an All-Carolina Conference player in 1973.

In 1974, Smith returned home to coach for four seasons at Great Mills High, where he had starred as a player, before moving on to coach Hoke County High in North Carolina for two years.

In 1980 he moved up to the college ranks, serving as an assistant coach with Virginia Commonwealth, South Carolina, and Kentucky through the 1980s. In 1991, Smith got his first head coaching job at Tulsa University and made a name for himself as a coach who could get his teams up for big games, particularly in the NCAA tournament. He took Tulsa to two Sweet Sixteen NCAA tournament finishes and two Missouri Valley Conference titles. He was named MVC Coach of the Year in 1994 and 1995.

After Tulsa, Smith took the reins at Georgia and led the Bulldogs to back-to-back NCAA tournament appearances, taking them to the Sweet Sixteen in 1996. In 1997, he took over as head coach at Kentucky after Rick Pitino stepped down, and led the Wildcats to the 1998 national championship in his first season.

Since his arrival at Kentucky, Smith has led the Wildcats to five SEC crowns, five SEC tournament titles, and six Sweet Sixteen finishes, in addition to one national championship. He also served as an assistant with the 2000 U.S. Olympic Team.

EMANUEL STEWARD—MOTOR CITY MAESTRO

Birth date: 1944 (exact date unknown)
Birthplace: Bottom Creek, West Virginia

Claim to fame: Founder of world-famous Kronk Boxing team and trainer of twenty-nine world champion fighters

Appropriate quote about Steward: "He's not just a good trainer, he's a surrogate father to his boxers. He took them off the street corners and taught them how to fight, and he always took care of them and got them started. Emanuel never took a cut of any purse smaller than $10,000."

—*Lou Duva, Hall of Fame boxing trainer*

Emanuel Steward was born in West Virginia and moved with his family to Detroit, Michigan, when he was eleven years old. The tough youngster earned respect in his new neighborhood by fighting his way through the city streets. Aat his mother's urging, he found his way inside a boxing gym and eventually won the Detroit Golden Gloves Championship in 1962 and the National Golden Gloves Bantamweight Championship in 1963.

After winning the Golden Gloves, Steward pulled away from boxing to begin raising his family, but in 1969, he was drawn back when his younger brother, James, asked Emanuel to teach him how to box. The brothers fared well. James won the Detroit Golden Gloves Championship in 1970 and Emanuel accepted the position of head boxing trainer at Kronk Gym in 1971—and the Kronk Boxing legend was born.

During the 1970s, Steward assembled the best stable of young fighters in the country, including future world champions Hilmer Kenty, Duane Thomas, and Thomas "Hit Man" Hearns. In 1980, Kenty and Hearns won world championships, and Kronk was recognized as the finest boxing gym in America, attracting the sport's brightest young stars.

Several members of the 1984 U.S. Olympic Team trained at Kronk, including Mark Breland, Tyrell Biggs, and Pernell Whitaker. All three fighters, and Kronk's own Frank Tate and Stevie McCrory, won gold medals at the 1984 games. Kronk fighters Milton Mcrory, Mike McCallum, and Jimmy Paul also won world championships in the 1980s.

In the 1990s, Steward developed more champions at Kronk and became a hired gun in the boxing world, sought out by top fighters to train for the biggest fights. He trained legends Julio Caesar Chavez, Evander Holyfield, and Oscar De La Hoya for championship fights, and guided Lennox Lewis to the undisputed heavyweight belt.

In 1980 Steward was selected by the Boxing Writers' Association of America as Manager of the Year and in 1997 was elected to the International Boxing Hall of Fame. Today, he continues to train fighters at Kronk Gym and enjoys a successful broadcasting career as a television commentator on HBO.

JOE TORRE—YANKEE SKIPPER

Birth date: July 18, 1940
Birthplace: Brooklyn, New York
Claim to fame: Managed Yankees to four World Series titles
Appropriate quote about Torre: "He just has that aura that makes you
   feel confident and comfortable to do well."

—*Alex Rodriguez, Yankees third baseman*

Joe Torre grew up with baseball. His older brother Frank played first base for the Milwaukee Braves from 1956 to 1960, helping them win the World Series in 1957. Joe broke into the major leagues with Milwaukee in 1960, when he was just twenty years old. As a catcher, he was an all-star from 1963 to 1967, winning the Gold Glove in 1965.

In 1969 he was traded to the St. Louis Cardinals for Orlando Cepeda, and two years later, in 1971, Torre had his best season as a player. He was moved to third base, and led the league in batting average (.363), RBIs (137), hits (230), and total bases (352), winning the National League's MVP honor. He was a four-time all-star with St. Louis, from 1970 to 1973, and was traded to the New York Mets in 1975.

In 1977, he retired as a player and took over as manager of the Mets, finishing his eighteen-year playing career with a .297 batting average, 252 home runs, 1,185 RBIs, and 2,342 hits.

Torre managed the Mets for six seasons, then the Atlanta Braves for three years, winning the NL Western Division title with Atlanta in 1982. After leaving the Braves in 1984, he worked as a broadcaster before being hired to manage the St. Louis Cardinals in 1990. He managed there for five years before moving on in 1996 to manage the New York Yankees.

Torre attained his greatest managerial success with the Yankees. In his first season, the Yanks won the World Series. In 1998, they won the Fall Classic again after setting a then American League record with 114 regular season wins, and won three Series in a row from 1998 to 2000 with stars like Derek Jeter, Bernie Williams, and Mariano Riviera.

Torre was named Manager of the Year in 1998, and he won six AL pennants and four World Series with the Yankees.

JOHN TORTORELLA—GO FOR IT

Birth date: June 24, 1958
Birthplace: Boston, Massachusetts
Claim to fame: Stanley Cup–winning head coach of the Tampa Bay
    Lightning
Appropriate quote about Tortorella: "He took over and was really hard
    on us. We didn't know why. But now we know. He had a plan."
                        —*Tampa Bay Lightning center Brad Richards*

John Tortorella is an enthusiastic straight-talker from Boston. He doesn't mince words, and says exactly what's on his mind. His team plays an aggressive, offensive style that is reflective of their coach's energetic personality.

Tortorella played in college at Salem State, then transferred to the University of Maine, where he was twice named an East Coast

Athletic Conference All-Star. After college he played in Sweden, then the Atlantic Coast Hockey League with Virginia, Hampton Roads, and Erie.

As a coach Tortorella is a proven winner at various levels. He was head coach of the Virginia Lancers (ACHL) in 1986–87 and 1987–88, winning the league championship and Coach of the Year honors in both seasons.

He then served as an assistant with the IHL Fort Wayne Komets in 1988 and the AHL New Haven Nighthawks in 1988–89. The next season he joined the Buffalo Sabres as an assistant and stayed with the Sabres' organization through the 1996–97 season. He coached their AHL team, the Rochester Americans, to the Calder Cup in 1996 and the AHL's best record in 1996–97.

In 1997, Tortorella came back up to the NHL as an assistant with the Phoenix Coyotes for two seasons. He then joined the New York Rangers for 1999–2000, serving as their interim head coach at the end of the 2000 season.

In 2001, he took over as head coach of the Tampa Bay Lightning and built his team with an explosive offense, blazing speed, and aggressive forechecking. The Lightning improved each season under Tortorella, making the play-offs following the 2002–03 season.

In 2003–04, the Lightning had their best season ever, with 46 wins and 106 points during the regular season. They rode their high-powered offense through the frenzy of the NHL play-offs, winning their first-ever Eastern Conference crown and Stanley Cup championship. Tortorella was named the NHL's Coach of the Year in 2004.

DICK VERMEIL—A BURNING DESIRE TO WIN

Birth date: October 30, 1936
Birthplace: Calistoga, California
Claim to fame: Super Bowl–winning head coach of the St. Louis Rams' "Greatest Show on Turf"

Appropriate quote about Vermeil: "He's a guy players will run through walls for, because he is an honest coach. He is not a BSer; he's a man of his word. He is genuine with not just the star players but with everybody on his roster."
— *former Rams linebacker and defensive captain London Fletcher*

Vermeil was born and raised in Calistoga, California, and attended Calistoga High School, where he was a four-sport star. After high school, he attended Napa Junior College for a year before moving on to San Jose State, where he played quarterback and earned his master's degree in physical education in 1959.

His coaching career began after graduation. He coached at various high schools and colleges through the 1960s, earning the rare distinction of being named Coach of the Year on each level he coached: high school, junior college, NCAA Division I, and later in the NFL.

Vermeil broke into the NFL in 1969 as the first-ever special teams coach under George Allen with the Los Angeles Rams. After bouncing back and forth between college and the pros for a couple of seasons, he coached the UCLA Bruins in 1974 and 1975, then landed his first head coaching gig in the NFL with the Philadelphia Eagles in 1976.

Before his arrival, the Eagles were awful, and hadn't had a winning season in ten years. Vermeil threw himself into his job, and was known to sleep at the stadium. His hard work paid off as he quickly turned the team around. In his third season, the Eagles posted a 9–7 record and made the play-offs for the first time since 1961. Vermeil was named NFC Coach of the Year for his efforts. Two years later, with players such as Ron Jaworski, Wilbert Montgomery, and Bill Bergey, they posted a franchise-best record of 12–4, and made it all the way to the Super Bowl. Vermeil was named NFL Coach of the Year.

The Eagles, however, lost Super Bowl XV, causing a downward spiral that Coach Vermeil agonized over so much so that after the

1982 season he stepped down as coach, citing burnout. He took a fourteen-year sabbatical from coaching, and became a television commentator, enjoying a successful broadcasting career.

In 1997, feeling as though he could handle the stress, Coach Vermeil took on another reconstruction project as head coach of the St. Louis Rams. The Rams had a streak of seven straight losing seasons and hadn't made the play-offs since 1988. Three years later, they won it all, taking Super Bowl XXXIV over the Tennessee Titans. The Rams' offense was dubbed the "Greatest Show on Turf" for their explosiveness, with quarterback Kurt Warner, running back Marshall Faulk, and wide receiver Torry Holt. Warner was named MVP of both the league and the Super Bowl, and Vermeil won NFL Coach of the Year honors for the second time.

After the Super Bowl victory, he retired again, only to return again as head coach of the Kansas City Chiefs in 2001. Vermeil retired from coaching after the 2005 season.

BILL WALSH—THE GENIUS

Birth date: November 30, 1931

Birthplace: Los Angeles, California

Claim to fame: Inventor of the "West Coast Offense" and winner of three Super Bowls as a head coach

Appropriate quote about Walsh: "There are a lot of things that I learned from Bill throughout my career, but I think the one thing that I continue throughout my life is that want to be perfect—the need for perfection. He pushed me and pushed us, especially the quarterback position which he was so proud of, to want to be perfect. And if you missed perfect, you end up with great, and that he could handle—but nothing else. He taught me to be the same way."

—*Joe Montana, Hall of Fame quarterback*

The San Francisco 49ers of the 1970s were one of the worst teams in the NFL, perennial losers who were never even in contention to make the play-offs. In 1979, after seventeen years as an assistant, Bill Walsh took over as their head coach. He had invented his own system, the "West Coast Offense," which was built on the short passing game. The new philosophy defied conventional football wisdom of the era that stated the need to run the ball effectively first in order to set up the passing game.

Walsh's aggressive new scheme relied on timing and accuracy, with the quarterback hitting receivers in stride on short, quick passing routes. This allowed the receivers, running at full speed, to make big plays after the catch. Walsh wanted to use the pass to set up the run. He drafted a young quarterback, Joe Montana, to implement his innovative game plan on the field.

In 1981, three years into Walsh's tenure, the 49ers met the heavily favored Dallas Cowboys in the NFC Championship Game. The Cowboys were "America's Team" and had dominated the conference during the 1970s. With time running out, Montana, under a heavy pass rush, floated a pass toward the back of the end zone. Wide receiver Dwight Clark snatched the ball out of the air with his fingertips and emphatically spiked it in the end zone for the touchdown. This play, now known as "the Catch," ended the Cowboys' run of excellence and commenced the 49ers' mastery of the new decade. They went on to their first of five Super Bowl victories—four of them in the 1980s.

In 1984, the offense exploded and the 49ers gelled, becoming arguably the single best team in the history of the league. They went a combined 18–1, including the play-offs, and won their second Super Bowl.

San Francisco became the league's most envied franchise and a model of business success in the corporate-minded environment of the 1980s. They were the team that other franchises emulated and aspired to be like. Walsh's winning ways permeated the entire organization.

LENNY WILKENS—COACHING DIPLOMAT

Birth date: October 28, 1937

Birthplace: Brooklyn, New York

Claim to fame: Winningest and losingest coach in NBA history

Appropriate quote about Wilkens: "Lenny has coached and can coach all kinds of different styles and be successful doing it. That's one of the things that's so great about him. I guess that's why he's in the Hall of Fame."

—Isiah Thomas, basketball Hall of Famer

Lenny Wilkens is one of the NBA's most well-traveled and successful figures. He overcame childhood poverty and racism to make it off Brooklyn's mean streets and into the Basketball Hall of Fame as both a player and coach.

Wilkens attended Boys High School in Brooklyn, and then Providence College in Rhode Island. He was a standout guard there, averaging nearly fifteen points a game throughout his college career, and earned second team All-American honors in his senior season in 1960.

Wilkens was drafted by the St. Louis Hawks in 1960, and became one of the league's best point guards. He was an intelligent playmaker, known for making the right decisions with the ball and getting his teammates involved in the action, and ranks ninth all-time in the NBA with 7,211 career assists. He averaged 16.5 points over his fifteen-year career, appeared in nine all-star games.

Wilkens also distinguished himself as a leader among his peers, serving as vice president of the players association from 1961 through 1969.

In 1969, he began his coaching career as player/head coach of the Seattle SuperSonics and served as player and coach in Seattle through the 1971–72 season. He then coached in Portland for two seasons before returning to Seattle in 1978. He led Seattle to the Finals in 1978, and returned in 1979, guiding the team to their only world championship.

Coach Wilkens has also made coaching stops with the Cleveland Cavaliers (1986–87 through 1992–93), Atlanta Hawks (1993–94 through 1999–2000), Toronto Raptors (2000–01 through 2002–03), and New York Knicks (2004–05).

He is enshrined in the Naismith Memorial Basketball Hall of Fame as both a player (1988) and coach (1998), a unique honor shared by only two other men, John Wooden and Bill Sharman. Wilkens has also served as president of the NBA Coaches Association.

JOHN WOODEN—THE WIZARD OF WESTWOOD

Birth date: October 14, 1910

Birthplace: Hall, Indiana

Claim to fame: Fabled UCLA coach who won ten NCAA men's basketball championships

Appropriate quote about Wooden: "John Wooden gave us the necessary tools to overcome the adversity and obstacles that he knew from the beginning would always be in our way."

—*Bill Walton, college and pro basketball great*

John Wooden was born and raised in the country's heartland, in the basketball haven of Indiana. As a youth he started shooting hoops into a tomato basket nailed onto the side of a barn on his family's farm. He developed into an all-state high school player, then went to college at Purdue, where he became a three-time All-American and the College Player of the Year in 1932. He was nicknamed the Indiana Rubber Man for his ability to bounce back up after throwing himself all over the court.

After college, Wooden taught and coached at the high school level for eleven years. He then coached at Indiana State University for two years, and in 1948, he took over as head coach at UCLA.

While at UCLA, Coach Wooden laid the foundation for what would become one of sports' greatest sustained dynasties. He built the character of his student-athletes through his Pyramid of Success, an illustration of building blocks he believes are essential to success in life and sports. He stressed fundamentals, such as using the backboard to improve shooting accuracy, and extended the length of practices to improve conditioning. The Bruins flourished under his guidance, becoming regular winners of the Pacific Coast Conference (later the Pac-10).

UCLA employed a 2–2–1 zone press defense that suffocated opponents, and offensively, they ran high-speed fast breaks in disciplined patterns. Operating at their peak, UCLA played and won as a cohesive unit.

In the 1960s and early 1970s, with their powder blue and gold uniforms and the white-haired, professorial-looking coach on the sidelines, they became an almost flawless winning machine, setting records that are nearly impossible to conceive of in team sports. Coach Wooden achieved the following milestones:

Ten national championships, including seven in a row (1966–73)

Four 30–0 seasons (1963–64, 1966–67, 1971–72, and 1972–73)

Eighty-eight consecutive victories

Thirty-eight straight NCAA tournament victories

A 149–2 home record

Nineteen Pac-10 championships

During this run, he won national Coach of the Year honors six times (1964, 1967, 1969, 1970, 1972, and 1973), was voted Man of the Year by the *Sporting News* in 1970, and *Sports Illustrated* Sportsman of the Year in 1973. He coached such basketball greats as Kareem Abdul Jabbar, Bill Walton, Gail Goodrich, and Jamaal Wilkes, and influenced an entire generation of coaches and players.

Coach Wooden is one of only three men enshrined in the Basketball Hall of Fame as both a player and coach (Bill Sharman and Lenny Wilkens are the others).

BIBLIOGRAPHY

Alexander, Rachel. "Bowman Has a Cupful of Stories," 1998. http://media.washingtonpost.com/wp-serv/sports/capitals/longterm/1998/stanleycup/articles/bowman15.htm (accessed 02/12/2006).

Arizona.edu. "Lute Olson's 500th Win Milestone in Life as Coach, Family Man, Private Citizen," 2001. wildcat.arizona.edu/papers/89/98/01_4_m.html (accessed 02/12/2006).

Armour, Nancy. "Bela Again in Gymnastics Spotlight," 2000. http://espn.go.com/olysummer00/gymnastics/s/2000/0918/755247.html (accessed 02/12/2006).

baseballlibrary.com. "Dusty Baker," 2002. http://www.baseballlibrary.com/baseballlibrary/ballplayers/B/Baker_Dusty.stm (accessed 03/26/2006).

baseballlibrary.com. "Mike Scioscia," 2005. http://www.baseballlibrary.com/baseballlibrary/ballplayers/S/Scioscia_Mike.stm (accessed 02/12/2006).

BBC Sport. "British Star on Life with the Tennis Elite," 2005. http://news.bbc.co.uk/sportacademy/hi/sa/tennis/features/newsid_3612000/3612214.stm (accessed 02/12/2006).

BengalsBlog. "On Marvin . . .," 2005. http://blogs.bengalszone.com/?cat=24 (accessed 02/12/2006).

Betz, Ed. "Pro Football 101 According to Herman Edwards," 2002. http://www.usatoday.com/sports/football/nfl/jets/2002-08-30-coach-edwards_x.htm (accessed 02/12/2006).

Bombulie, Jonathan. "Hawkeyes Boast Wrestling Dynasty," 2005. http://www.collegian.psu.edu/archive/1996_jan-dec/01/01-11-96cm/01-11-96m01-006.htm (accessed 02/12/2006).

Boston.com. "She's a Role Player," 2004. http://www.boston.com/sports/basketball/articles/2004/05/14/shes_a_role_player?pg=2 (accessed 02/13/2006).

Carucci, Vic. "Montana's Induction 'a Beginning,'" 2000. http://www.nfl.com/news/hof/montana.html (accessed 02/12/2006).

Cnnsi.com. "New Woman in Charge," 2000. http://sportsillustrated.cnn.com/soccer/news/2000/01/18/us_coach/ (accessed 2/12/2006).

Cornfield, Josh. "Every Player Has Meant Something," 2001. http://www.temple.edu/temple_news/chaney/players.html (accessed 02/12/2006).

Cristodero, Damian. "Tortorella Honored," 2004. http://www.sptimes.com/2004/06/11/Lightning/Tortorella_honored.shtml (accessed 02/12/2006).

Dixon, Oscar. "Strike, Too? Labor Rumblings Cloud Future," 2002. http://www.usatoday.com/sports/basketba/wnba/stories/2002-07-12-wnba-labor.htm (accessed 03/26/2006).

Ecachockeyleague.com. "Philadelphia Flyers Coach Ken Hitchcock to Volunteer to Coach Princeton Men's Hockey Team," 2004. http://www.ecachockeyleague.com/news/men/princeton-hitchcock (accessed 02/12/2006).

ESPN.com. "Giants Raise the Bahr on 49ers," 1999. http://espn.go.com/nfl/playoffs98/news/1999/990112/01042137.html (accessed 03/26/2006).

espn.com. "Kentucky Signs Coach to Eight Year Extension," 2003. http://sports.espn.go.com/espn/print?id=1541050&type=news (accessed 02/12/2006).

Falsani, Cathleen. "You Can Be a Christian and Be Hard-Nosed," *Chicago Sun Times.* 2004. http://www.suntimes.com/output/falsani/cst-nws-spirit13.html (accessed 03/26/2006).

fightingmaster.com. "Angelo Dundee," 2003. http://www
.fightingmaster.com/trainers/dundee/ (accessed 02/12/2006).

detnews.com. "Dungy, Colts Are a Good Fit," 2002.
www.detnews.com/2002/lions/0206/21/e11d-518748.htm (accessed
02/12/2006).

Greenstein, Teddy. "It's All Yours, Dusty," 2002. http://
www.chicagotribune.com/news/local/cs-021115cubshirebaker
,0,7808072.story?page=2&coll=chi-news-hed (accessed 02/12/2006).

Hannon, Kerry. "Tennis Coach Brings Lessons from the Court,"
2004. http://www.keepmedia.com/pubs/USATODAY/2004/09/13/
577704?extID=10026 (accessed 02/12/2006).

Hilton, Lisette. "Auerbach's Celtics Played as a Team," 2005.
http://espn.go.com/classic/biography/s/Auerbach_Red.html
(accessed 02/11/2006).

Howard, Theresa. "Torre Goes to Bat for His Team," 2004. http://
www.usatoday.com/money/companies/management/2004-08-09-
torre_x.htm (accessed 02/12/2006).

ibhof.com. "Lou Duva," 1998. http://www.ibhof.com/duva.htm
(accessed 02/12/2006).

Jamison, Steve. "The Joys of the Journey," 2003. http://
www.coachwooden.net/thejourney.html (accessed 03/26/2006).

Katz, Andy. "For Olson, Family Has Always Come First," 2002.
http://espn.go.com/ncb/columns/katz_andy/1437423.html (accessed
03/26/2006).

Kertes, Tom. "Knicks Deeper and Improved, Says Thomas," 2004.
http://www.nba.com/knicks/news/improved_041001.html (accessed
02/12/2006).

Korte, Tim. "Nebraska Coach Tom Osborne Retires," 1997.
http://chronicle.augusta.com/stories/121097/mike.shtml (accessed
02/12/2006).

Lancaster, Marc. "No Sense of Urgency for Lewis," 2003.
http://www.cincypost.com/bengals/2003/lewis01-18-2003.html
(accessed 03/26/2006).

Lurie, Mike. "Brian Billick to Deliver UMB Commencement Address," 2005. http://www.gbc.org/Member%20news/052005-UMB-commencement.html (accessed 02/12/2006).

Mileur, Ray. "The Great White Hope," 2004. http://www.thestlcardinals.com/thegreatwhitehope.html (accessed 02/12/2006).

Miller, Ted. "Storm Coach: A Woman of Stature," 2004. http://seattlepi.nwsource.com/wnba/192265_donovan24.html (accessed 02/12/2006).

Okino, Betty. "Betty Okino's Olympic Report," 2000. http://www.sportshollywood.com/gymnastics1.html (accessed 03/26/2006).

Perry, Michael. "Xavier Must Contend with Temple Zone," 1999. http://www.enquirer.com/xavier/1999/02/14/xu_xavier_must_contend.html (accessed 03/26/2006).

Pitoniak, Scott. "Winning Is Never Out of Style with Vermeil," 2003. http://www.democratandchronicle.com/sports/columns/10251Q25SHD_scott25_columns.shtml (accessed 02/12/2006).

Puma, Mike. "Parcells Made Struggling Franchises into Winners," 2005. http://espn.go.com/classic/biography/s/Parcells_Bill.html (accessed 02/12/2006).

Rousos, Rick, and Mike Cobb. "Papa 'Nole: The Life and Times of Bobby Bowden," 2005. http://www.theledger.com/static/bowden/day9. htm (accessed 02/12/2006).

Scott, Richard. "The Survivor," 2005. http://www.americanfootballmonthly.com/Subaccess/Magazine/2000/July'00/fisher.html (accessed 02/12/2006).

Silver, Michael. "Miracle Worker," 2000. http://sportsillustrated.cnn.com/features/cover/news/2000/11/15/moments_miracle/ (accessed 03/26/2006).

Sportsillustrated.cnn.com. "Cubs Hire Baker," 2002. http://sportsillustrated.cnn.com/baseball/news/2002/11/15/baker_hired_cubs_ap/ (accessed 03/26/2006).

Stellino, Vito. "I Know I'm Good," *Football Digest,* 2001. http://www.gradewinner.com/p/articles/mi_m0FCL/is_5_30/ai_67831652 (accessed 03/26/2006).

storm.wnba.com. "Storm Name Anne Donovan Head Coach," 2002. http://www.wnba.com/storm/news/donovan_021218.html (accessed 02/12/2006).

Strauss, Chris. "Leading Man," *Pittsburgh Magazine.* 2005. http://www.wqed.org/mag/features/0805/cowher1.shtml (accessed 02/12/2006).

Telegraphindia.com. "Of Technique and Human Touch—Coach Gilbert Brings Out the Best in Roddick," 2003. http://www.telegraphindia.com/1030912/asp/sports/story_2358287.asp (accessed 03/26/2006).

Walton, Bill. "John Wooden, Like UCLA, Simply the Best," 2001. http://www.billwalton.com/wooden.html (accessed 02/12/2006).

Wnba.com. "Mercury Name Carrie Graf Head Coach," 2004. http://www.wnba.com/mercury/news/graf_040413.html (accessed 02/12/2006).

PHOTO CREDITS